# Designing Creative Portfolios

# Gregg Berryman

THOMSON

COURSE TECHNOLOGY ™

www.courseilt.com

**Library of Congress**
**Cataloging-in-Publication Data**

Berryman, Gregg, 1942–
    Designing creative portfolios / Gregg
Berryman.
      p.    cm.
    Includes bibliographical references.
    ISBN 1-56052-113-9 :
    1. Art portfolios—Design. 2. Graphic
arts—Marketing.
    I. Title.
    NC1001.B47  1992
    741.6'068'8—dc20        92-39103
                              CIP

05 06  12 11 10

For more information contact:
Course Technology
25 Thomson Place
Boston, MA 02210

ISBN 1-56052-113-9

# Contents

# Acknowledgments

Dedicated to the Graphic Design Alumni
of California State University, Chico
for your dedication, esprit de corps,
professionalism and achievements.

A special thanks to my wife Phyllis
for her loving support and technical
input. Phil Gerould, Publisher, of Crisp
Publications has my lasting gratitude
for his patience and encouragement
which extended far beyond the norm.
The sage advice and comments of
the many designers, educators and
placement professionals have helped
add relevance and dimension to
this book.

Design: Gregg Berryman
Input: Phyllis Berryman
Editor: Kay Kepler
Illustration: Chris Ficken, Phil Quinn
Typography: ExecuStaff
Printer: Von Hoffmann Graphics, Inc.
Type: American Typewriter, Helvetica

# Introduction

**An employer will spend five minutes looking over what has taken you years to accomplish. All of your effort must be focused on quickly communicating what you think about design and yourself, without reservation.**
Craig Frazier
Principal
Frazier Design
San Francisco

**Let your obsession with design show. I have always liked to hire fanatics.**
Sumner Stone
Principal
Stone Type Foundry, Inc.
Palo Alto, CA

Creative professionals view the portfolio as the single most important employment tool. Supported by an effective resume, strong recommendations and interviewing skills, the portfolio or "book" is your ticket for admission into challenging, creative positions. It offers hard evidence of problem solving and answers the "show-me" demands of employers.

This book defines a special kind of portfolio, the *creative portfolio.* Employers of creative professionals tend to be articulate, extremely selective and set high standards. They work under tight deadlines. These busy professionals know how to communicate visually and verbally and expect the same from those they interview. An average portfolio will not impress them. Only the bright, imaginative, creative portfolio will spark a positive response.

The creative portfolio needs to be exceptional. It must demonstrate how you think and communicate your thoughts while positioning you above the hordes of job seekers in competition for the most desirable positions. Your book must clearly articulate your uniqueness and connect your talents with the needs of a potential employer. Your creative portfolio holds the power to make each interview a special event.

Creative professionals assemble several portfolios in the span of a career. An application portfolio is required to enter top design schools. The internship portfolio is necessary to help you get stimulating part-time positions while you study or during summer vacation. An exit portfolio measures the quality and dimension of your undergraduate study. It guides you into the marketplace and helps jump-start your career. Graduate schools of design require a portfolio for admission to advanced degree candidacy. As your design career develops, your professional portfolio includes updated samples and projects in progress.

The creative portfolio should not be a static package but an evolving collection of concepts, solutions and samples. It must identify you, enhance your credibility and project an honest profile of your capabilities. It should clarify your problem-solving skills and technical knowledge. Above all, the creative portfolio needs to demonstrate your promise and potential for growth to each target studio, agency or corporation.

The primary goal of this book is to provide a user-friendly portfolio reference for designers beginning their careers. Contents will help set a benchmark of portfolio information useful for educators, counselors and employers in creative visual professions. Readers are challenged to envision the portfolio-building process conceptually, rather than as a formula. By considering the portfolio as a distinct design problem, you are encouraged to develop an appropriate solution unique to you.

# Employer Perceptions

Leading design studios, agencies and offices are very particular when hiring. Most are interested primarily in the cream of the crop. You need to clearly demonstrate that if you do not now fit this category you soon will. Employers demand the solid educational background provided by a recognized university or art school program. They realize that "skills-only" training will limit the future growth of a young designer. Only with a solid foundation in design history, theory and methodology will employees be able to absorb technology, interpret culture and communicate effectively.

Most employers have a different perception of "design talent" than your own. Designers often equate creativity with elegant visual form, sophisticated color systems and highly personal illustration. Employers see a bigger picture. They place an equal or greater value on consistency, competitiveness, reliability, dedication, integrity and interpersonal skills. Clients rate design output on yet another scale. A client's primary concern is the delivery of a design assignment on or before deadline. Next, they consider how the design piece affects the corporate bottom line. Clients are then concerned with the visual aesthetics of the assignment.

Successful design firms take hiring seriously. The process is time consuming and a good personnel decision is critical or the process must be repeated, often at great effort and expense. Over time, filling a design position represents a huge financial investment. While most beginning salaries are moderate, employers must supplement them with mandated benefits including social security and workers' compensation. Perks such as health coverage, paid parking, profit-sharing or health club memberships also increase the "invisible salary."

Employers assume that it will take time to bring young designers up to speed, while they absorb office procedures and learn technical systems. If you can shorten this accommodation period, your value, to the company will increase. The sooner it is apparent that you are helping the firm make a profit, the faster you will be promoted.

Kris Edwards, president of Edwards and Shepard Agency, New York City design recruiters, has evolved her "CREPTT" formula for designers who are serious about retaining their position with a creative firm. This accurately mirrors employers' perception of employee value.

**C   is for Creativity.** You can't survive without it—keep up with the times.
**R   is for Reliability.** Show up on time, and be the one to be counted upon.
**E   is for Enthusiasm.** Love what you do and what your employer does.
**P   is for Performance.** Get it done, do it right and appreciate constructive criticism.
**T   is for Trustworthiness.** Be loyal, devoted and limit personal matters at work.
**T   is for Teamplaying.** Work with others, help others, and be part of a whole.

**The single most important ingredient to a successful designer/client relationship is for the designer to understand that the client is expecting a problem to be solved in exchange for money . . . a business problem generally. The designer is retained to aid in the successful prosecution of the client's business interests . . . not to develop creative concepts for the intrinsic value of the art itself.**
William G. Townsend
Principal
William Townsend
Company
Sacramento, CA

**A beautiful portfolio will open many doors. But well-chosen words to accompany your presentation will be the deciding factor when it comes to getting hired. I look for designers who can talk beyond the design. What is the client trying to accomplish? Why do you think your design achieves that goal? How will you prepare your design for the printer? These days, success in the graphic design business means more than winning a beauty contest.**
Paul Page
Principal
Page Design, Inc.
Sacramento, CA

# Design
# Attitude

Measure yourself against the character-istics of successful graphic designers. As individuals, most are extremely curious with diverse interests. They tend to be well read outside the field of design. A broad liberal arts background contrib-utes to their worldliness as does travel abroad. An awareness of the creative visual disciplines of architecture, indus-trial design, landscape architecture and fashion design helps them place graphic design in context. Fine arts and art history serve as important stimuli.

Top designers develop a genuine love of design. They share a strong belief and conviction in their work, honed through sacrifice and commitment to excellence. They are self-critical and remain open-minded to constructive criticism. Many are driven to live by design. Design inno-vators assign their profession a very high priority in their existence. Assertive and confident designers tend to thrive in the most competitive circumstances.

Graphic designers work in close collab-oration with others. Solid team players prosper. Selfish prima donnas tend to contaminate work environments already charged with high energy, stress and tight deadlines. A positive good-natured attitude helps contribute to the total team effort. Designers with genuine enthu-siasm and outgoing personalities are fun to work with. If they are also courteous, have listening skills and possess a sense of humor, so much the better.

**Study the history of art and design; knowing the past makes for a creative future. New and interesting concepts can only come from expanding on past experiences. Your board skills will make the above live or die.**
John J. Sorbie
Professor Emeritus
Colorado State University
Fort Collins, CO

**Let's assume your work has good concept, fine execution and is presented impeccably —the only other ingredient necessary is an enthusiastic attitude. You want potential employers to know that you want to design for them.**
Russell Leong
Principal
Russell Leong Design
Palo Alto, CA

**Reading, travel and broad-based cultural experiences should be required continuing education for design graduates.**
Steve Barbaria
Principal
Tackett-Barbaria Design
Sacramento, CA

# Conceptual Strategies

Strong conceptual ability is necessary for reaching the upper plateau of graphic design, as it is for all the creative professions. Those who can generate abundant fresh ideas and communicate them with clarity and elegance rise to the top. Consistent application of critical thinking skills and problem-solving methodology helps designers produce rich alternative solutions.

A foundation of communication theory provides the designer with a means to explore the nooks and crannies of the creative process. Worldliness and cultural awareness developed through reading and travel add rich texture to design solutions. Strong intuition is a characteristic of leading design innovators and supports their courage to take chances.

Concepts born in historical context help the designer to make relevant connections based on understanding rather than naivety. Empathy with the needs of clients adds validity to the creative process. Top designers are able to retain a global view of the problem at hand while detailing solutions. An ease of visualizing "big ideas" characterizes most successful design professionals.

Graphic designers must be able to subject each problem to careful analysis . . . breaking the whole into separate parts. They also learn to apply synthesis, which combines two or more dissimilar ideas into a single form. Designers use both inductive thinking (moving from problem specifics to a general concept) and deductive thinking (from general to specific). Synectics, a creative process incorporating both analogies and metaphors to stimulate ideas is also useful to designers.

Designers must be able to conduct effective research. Deciding *what* to investigate is critical. Research can be as simple as a conversation with a client or a field visit. It might also involve interpreting complex market research. Framing a problem in unique terms improves your opportunity for an original solution.

The creative process is only complete when ideas are recorded for evaluation. Designers often generate lists of words to stimulate images. By drawing on verbal descriptors, synonyms, literal meanings, slang, phonics, clichés and abstractions they expand design alternatives. Graphic designers need to be able to write about their ideas and discuss them. Concepts must be compared, edited and translated into forms meaningful to clients and audiences. Articulate communication is an accurate measure of visual intelligence.

Conceptual strategies are recorded and tested by graphic designers through an interactive visual process which involves seeing, imagining and drawing. Each of the three activities stimulates and activates the other. Architects, product designers, city planners, fashion designers, landscape architects and interior designers also share this process, most often through tracing and overlays. This visual thinking continuum is a potent incubator of alternative solutions.

Good thinking is as important as good design. Beyond the design's appearance, I look for the individual's ability to demonstrate an understanding of the problem, to state the design objectives and to explain how the solution meets those objectives.
Greg Silveria
Design Director
Group Four Design
Avon, CT

I'm looking for ideas—concept is more important than execution. If it is a poor idea I don't care how good it looks. I want to see how you think and can expand a concept into other pieces.
Craig Hedges
Vice President
Director of Design
Ketchum Advertising
Los Angeles

Attractive and polished portfolios attract my attention, but the core of my review will always be the idea and its execution. The portfolio must show me how you think. Beautiful design is effective only if it solves the problem and communicates.
Frank Burris
Art Director
Kramer Carton
Sacramento, CA

# Drawing Competence

**Can you draw and sketch? Many designers forget to demonstrate this most basic ability. Include exhibits that illustrate your skills in concept visualization and rendering.**
Steve Holler
Creative Director
Raychem Corporation
Menlo Park, CA

**I like to see a small, tidy documentation of a design process included in a portfolio. To see the evolution of an idea from thumbnails to fruition gives me an instant read on a designer's thinking process and discipline. And of course keep it short.**
Bobbi Long
Principal
Wish You Were Here
San Francisco

**Show neatly organized development ideas, preferably pencil or marker (or laser print-outs). These idea sketches are always helpful to demonstrate your thinking process, and more importantly, sketches reveal your drawing abilities.**
Doyald Young
Principal
Doyald Young
Graphic Design
Sherman Oaks, CA

Graphic designers need to develop extraordinary eye/hand skills. The ability to draw is fundamental to translating concepts and clarifies the communication process. Great designers master the language of drawing to indicate their thoughts. Leonardo, Picasso and Frank Lloyd Wright developed their genius from the foundation of masterful drawing.

Drawing is essential to translate ideas for evaluation. Designers should master a broad spectrum of specialized drawing techniques. Visual brainstorming, flow diagrams, graphic models and decision trees help to bridge the distance between raw concepts and reality. Strategic drawing probes the initial phases of the creative process. Designers utilize drawing overlays for quick modification of conceptual drawings . . . the act of tissuing yields bountiful results.

Drawing to translate information is critical to understanding. Designers communicate with audiences through charts, graphs, tables and maps. They learn to integrate symbolic language with drawing to clarify distance, space and time. Graphic designers build their drawing vocabulary by absorbing the principles of proportion, view projection, rotation, cross-section and perspective. Combined with form translation through line, volume, surface and light, designers use drawing to stimulate ideation, memory and experience. In the words of the great British sculptor Henry Moore "Drawing concentrates knowledge."

Accurate freehand drawing demands keen observation and reflects the designer's ability to see in a special way. Lucid idea sketches stimulate communication with others on the design team. Clients must view precise comprehensive visualizations to clearly understand the design intent. Without strong drawing, visual ambiguities tend to compromise the problem-solving process. Many superb ideas have been rejected by clients confused by distorted drawing and weak presentation.

Renown designer/illustrator Milton Glaser advises young designers about drawing in *The School of Visual Arts Guide to Careers.* "I don't think there's anything more wonderful than finding out you did a drawing that was better than you thought you could do . . . I am still astonished at what happens through drawing. I just can't believe it." The magic of solid drawing is tightly interwoven with the creative process. Your skills should be kept fresh through practice, application, experimentation and coursework to help expose you to the many dimensions of drawing. To continue to draw improves both your competence and confidence which in turn stimulates heightened creativity.

While the computer continues to grow in importance as a creative tool, designers must not neglect the development of strong drawing fundamentals. Computers with sophisticated programs are powerful assistants, but cannot substitute for your human touch and conceptual vitality. Renderings and illustrations produced with the help of computers depend on your drawing foundation to achieve viability.

# Typographic Insight

Developing strong typographic skills reflects a reverence for the written and printed word. Virtually all graphic solutions involve information that must be translated into typography. Designers need to treat typography as a lifelong study, building sensitivity through exposure, experimentation and experience.

Committed designers must absorb the principles of both traditional and contemporary typography. The rich history of typography mirrors the development of the arts of civilization. To neglect the past and focus only on typographic fashion is short-sighted. To be driven only by the technology of the computer is limiting. Doyald Young, the Los Angeles master of typographic logotypes advises designers to "Avoid the trendy type cliche. Choose well designed types or those with a good track record. Remember classic types may be arranged in layouts so as to appear contemporary. But arrange them so that the reader gets the message easily."

Beginning graphic designers need to master the terminology of type. They must understand how typesetting systems have evolved and the technology of this evolution. A knowledge of the history of type and the classification of typefaces is expected. Old Style, Transitional, Modern, Slab Serif, Scripts and Ornamental styles compose broad categories of type from which the designer can draw for specific applications. Designers need to develop the knowledge to mine the rich lode of thousands of available type faces.

Researching the life and times of significant type designers lends depth and meaning to typography. Many successful graphic designers adopt inspirational typographic heroes like Gill, Tschichold, Goudy or Zapf as they develop a passion for their work.

Graphic designers must understand audiences and how typographic messages reach them. Designers should learn to control typographic legibility and the external factors that influence it. They establish typographic hierarchy to effectively interpret verbal messages.

Type can stand alone and become the sole subject of graphic expression. It can support and complete a message in conjunction with photos or illustration. Type can add finish detail and meaning to complex information. Designers need to be able to specify and apply type as mastheads, headlines, subheads, pull quotes, blurbs, body type, sidebars, captions, callouts, folios and credits. They must construct meaningful layouts to guide readers through the broad spectrum of publications.

Typography helps drive page structure, reading paths and layout systems that add clarity to information. The relationship of typography to icons, photography and illustration demands careful study by graphic designers. Typography must also be understood in the context of outdoor, wayfinding, retail and electronic environments.

The nuances of typography separate the exceptional from the ordinary. Designers learn to vary type size, weight and scale with appropriate contrast to affect the mood of an audience. The emotional content and voice of type can be adjusted to add pace and resonance to a poster, page, ad or television graphic.

**Showing excellent typographic skills is most important. Remember that unlike photography or illustration, typography is involved in virtually every design project.**
Bob Dahlquist
Principal
Bob's Haus
Sacramento, CA

**I look for a practical understanding of typography. A knowledge and appreciation of classical typographic treatments, organizational ability and basic type skills are essential to the communication of even the wildest concept. Before one can create "bad" typography, one must have a thorough understanding of good typography.**
Tony Auston
Design Director
Colona, Farrell:
Design Associates
St. Helena, CA

**I look for work that shows sensitivity to type, demonstrates your ability to think and execute, and is compatible with the work of my studio.**
Sandra McHenry
Principal
Sandra McHenry Design
San Francisco

## Word Software

Microsoft Word®
Claris MacWrite®
WordPerfect®

## Layout Software

Quark Xpress®
Aldus PageMaker®
Corel Ventura®

## Draw Software

Macromedia Freehand®
Adobe Illustrator®
CorelDraw®
Altsys Fontographer®
Fractual Design Painter®

## Image Edit Software

Adobe Photoshop®
Corel PhotoPaint®

## Presentation Software

Aldus Persuasion®
Gold Disc Astound®
MacroMedia Action®
Microsoft PowerPoint®

## MultiMedia Software

Asymetrix Toolbook®
HyperCard®
MacroMedia Authorware®
MacroMedia Director®

## 3-D Software

Alias Sketch®
MacroMedia 3-D®
Ray Dream Designer®
Strata Studio Pro®

## Video Software

Adobe Premiere®
Avid VideoShop®

---

**Designers need to hone their computer skills as much as ever, if not more so—we're now talking about not just using computers but using them well. We need designers who can design a page that won't choke our service bureau's imagesetter. I'll ask to see not only a printed portfolio but also the files that created it.**

Jake Widman
Editor
Publish Magazine
San Francisco

---

**Fluent computer skills are prerequisite in today's design environment. Be prepared to demonstrate your design process . . . thumbnails through finished electronic art. Chart an efficient path using the appropriate software program. Include a demonstration disc as part of your portfolio. Don't be afraid to deviate from the computer if traditional tools yield quicker and superior results.**

David Bacigalupi
Art Director
MMS Design
Sebastopol, CA

---

**Present work that demonstrates your ability to work creatively with type— not just display type but also with text type. This is what sets a good designer apart. Show up-to-date work that demonstrates personal growth. Stay current with computer hardware and software and display these skills in your portfolio.**

Susan Merritt
Principal
CWA, Inc.
San Diego, CA

---

Computers play an important role in graphic design. While some of the most innovative professionals reject the computer, a larger number embrace it. Computers help relieve some of the drudgery of repetitive tasks. These tools help designers speed up the exploration of visual alternatives and free them to spend additional time on the creative process.

Understanding how computers integrate the design/production process is essential. Graphic designers should have a working knowledge of four types of software. Word processing software is used to generate and edit text. Draw/Paint software helps produce refined illustrations, icons and trademarks. Image editing software allows designers to scale, retouch and combine photographs. Page layout software is useful for creating pages, spreads and entire publications.

Digital prepress technology allows graphic designers to assume much of the traditional responsibility of typesetters and printers. Computers help cut costs and speed up the prepress process, adding precision while providing paper, film and even direct plate output.

Graphic designers need to acquire an understanding of animation, multimedia and interactive media. Presentation software is used to produce color slides for learning packages and product promotion. Three-dimensional software enhances the study and rendering of products, architecture and environments. Multimedia software helps integrate type, photos, sound and video for educational, corporate and institutional clients.

# Business Awareness

To rise above the norm, graphic designers should develop a general understanding of the business of design. A good foundation includes a grasp of the basic principles of marketing, advertising, finance and management. Designers who can see from the client's perspective have a genuine advantage. An ability to understand project budgets and how they affect work flow is valuable. Efficient time management and the capability to work quickly add value to the designer.

Young designers must grasp how studios, agencies and corporations are organized and how each differs. You need to understand the strategies employed by each creative group to meet its business overhead, price its design services and earn profits. Once you achieve a business awareness by understanding personal responsibilities to the design effort, your career will gain meaning.

Solid writing contributes immensely to the design team effort. Graphic designers must be capable of generating intelligent project briefs, business letters, proposals and transmittals. Copywriting skills are important. Designers often write, rewrite and edit headlines, captions and body copy.

Design presentations determine the ultimate success of a proposed solution and involve both speaking and interpersonal communication skills. Clients must be persuaded to buy into design proposals in the language of marketing rather than the esoteric vocabulary of design. Truly gifted presenters develop an easy rapport with clients, master the art of persuasion and often move to the top levels of design management.

**In presenting to an ad agency, I'm a firm believer in having your portfolio and presentation combine art and business. Don't get too cutesy-clever or you won't be taken seriously. Of course, if you're too grey and dry, your work won't stand out. Know the agency's work style. In presenting, tie your strengths into what they're looking for.**
Greg Chew
Creative Director
DAE Media, Inc.
San Francisco

**Let something in your portfolio demonstrate to me that you will be a valuable employee for my company. Can you use the Macintosh computer? Include a piece of work that proves it . . . using a typeface that I like.**
Brian Burch
Art Director
Burch Design Group
Sacramento, CA

**As a professional, design solutions have to develop quickly. The day-to-day business side of what we do demands so much attention . . . client relations, accounting, new business development. Smart business sense is critical to producing great design.**
Greg Berman
Principal
Sargent + Berman
Los Angeles

# Employment Locations

First ask yourself "Where do I want to live?" Begin your search by narrowing your geographic target. It is virtually impossible to explore the entire USA, the Southwest, or all of California in a single effort. Focus your attention on the top media markets. Several publishers annually survey metropolitan areas and rank them according to quality-of-life criteria. The economy, cost of living, housing, health care, climate, air quality, crime rate, fine arts, recreation and quality of schools enter into the index.

Only the major markets have concentrations of large clients, good budgets and top creative personnel. You can change jobs without changing cities. New York City represents the market extreme with a concentration of nearly 20,000 design and advertising positions.

The magnet suburbs found near large cities offer an alternative. Palo Alto (near San Francisco), Evanston (near Chicago) Stamford, Connecticut (near New York City) are centers that attract corporations, agencies and studios but offer a more relaxed lifestyle than nearby cities.

Small markets afford more limited opportunity to launch your career. Lesser competition, reduced salary and marginal project budgets can slow your professional growth. If you accept your first position in a small market, pay your dues and then move up in a year or so. Experienced designers often thrive in small markets, but after they have competed at the national level.

Finally, once you select a market receptive to your talents, visit a time or two to take its pulse. Align the lifestyle, weather and economics with your preferences. Move to your target city while you interview, budgeting for a two or three month stay.

# Employment
# Alternatives

Develop a sound strategy to help you decide the kind of position that best fits you. If your creative portfolio shows breadth, your alternatives increase. A highly specialized portfolio might limit your horizons.

Corporate design involves working exclusively for one company, university, hospital or government agency as a staff designer. Projects involve corporate collateral, visual identity translation, publications, sales literature, event promotion and employee information. Large organizations tend to hire for the long term, pay well, offer benefit packages and require teamwork. Some designers find the corporate hierarchy stifling. Others thrive by extending the historical visual excellence of such corporations as IBM, Apple, Mobil, Raychem, Polaroid and John Deere.

Advertising agencies offer opportunities to create in both print and television. Designers work on teams alongside copywriters and creative directors. They may choose to serve local clients in small markets or join giant AAAA agencies representing sponsors in the national and international media. Advertising is generally fast-paced with tight deadlines. Designers with creative spontaneity do well in this persuasive profession. Advertising agencies richly compensate top creative talent; however frequent job changes may be common due to account movement and economic cycles.

Graphic design consultants vary in size from large firms with hundreds of employees that market internationally to smaller offices of five or so in regional markets. They work for a range of corporate and institutional clients in much the same manner as architects. Projects include corporate identity, packaging, sign systems, exhibits, annual reports and collateral. This process involves collaborative team design. Financial compensation varies with the scale of the market and the size of clients.

Publishing has a rich historical tradition. Book designers work with authors, editors, illustrators and photographers on textbooks, novels, reference literature and childrens' books. They create formats, cover designs and promotional materials. Some designers focus on limited edition publishing using traditional letterpress printing. Most book designers work with educational, trade and business publishing firms. Others are employed in the scholarly university press to publish research.

Magazine designers direct illustrators, photographers and free-lancers to produce consumer, business and specialty publications. Thousands of magazines are produced in every imaginable category each week, month and quarter. Top magazine designers are expert with type and sequential images. Magazine design positions are concentrated in the major markets but exist in every state.

Graphic designers employed by daily and weekly newspapers create section pages, features, information graphics and marketing promotions. Newspaper designers thrive on short deadlines. They work closely with writers and editors to interpret local, national and international events.

**A portfolio is a solution to a problem. A student should first clarify her/his short-range and preferably long-range career objectives and then, and not before, select (and probably re-do) the most appropriate pieces. Then, the student should design a presentation format that will best help them get the job they want. In my portfolio class, I have students project their futures by picturing, through their own research, what kind of life they can see themselves living five years in the future.**
Sam Smidt
Professor/Designer
San Jose State University
San Jose, CA

**Every design firm has its own unique needs for prospective designers. A portfolio with inappropriate concepts and/or skills will not be well received, no matter how spectacular the work. And remember, your worst piece will have greater impact than your best.**

Charles W. Jennings
Professor/Dept. Chair
Dept. of Art and Design
Cal Poly State University
San Luis Obispo, CA

Environmental graphic designers create sign systems, banners, vehicle identity, museum installations, retail spaces and trade show exhibits. These design specialists interact with architects, fabricators and contractors. Particular strength in three-dimensional design, wayfinding and space planning is necessary. Budgets are large and earning potential is high in this specialty.

Entertainment graphics firms are located near the media production centers in New York, Los Angeles, San Francisco and Chicago. Designers produce print, television, film and video graphics for networks, movie studios and media production companies. They also create promotional and licensed materials including posters, clothing, toys and related collateral.

Free-lance graphic designers are employed as independent contractors for a variety of design studios and agencies. They work inside design offices on a project or part-time basis. Sometimes they work in an office at home and communicate with design directors through fax and computer modem. Free-lancers, as sub-contractors, do not receive employee benefits, insurance or vacations. Many young designers find free-lance work an attractive way to sample a variety of employers and work environments. Outstanding free-lancers in busy markets are in great demand and are often richly rewarded.

Multimedia design offers a fertile direction for graphic designers in the areas of education, corporate training and entertainment. To be effective, designers need to communicate information, integrate video and help users navigate easily. Multimedia is usually a collaborative effort much like producing a film. Designers interested in animation, film, video and the leading edges of technology tend to thrive in multimedia design.

Design education at the college, art school or university level offers career opportunities. Academia requires the MFA degree in design and significant professional experience. Rising to the top rank of Professor demands consistent research and recognition over many years. Part-time lecture and adjunct appointments are available for outstanding design professionals.

Other opportunities for graphic designers exist with audiovisual studios, architecture firms, marketing consultants, public relations agencies, zoological gardens, sports franchises, amusement complexes, convention centers, shopping malls, political consultants and financial institutions. World Fairs, Olympic Games, political conventions, music festivals, trade shows and sports tournaments require event marketing graphics on a per-project basis.

The spectrum of graphic design positions is ever widening. Graphic designers are percolating down into smaller markets. Competition ranges from stiff to fierce for the best clients and positions. Your creative portfolio must show you at the very peak of your creative power to achieve your target position.

# Portfolio Planning

Plan your portfolio in response to employer perceptions of designers. Explore techniques to present evidence of your conceptual power, typographic innovation, drawing skills and computer competency. Thorough portfolio planning will help you reach your goal with maximum efficiency.

Envision hiring a talented designer to create your portfolio. What kind of product would you be willing to pay for? Certainly you would expect an honest audit of your design samples, an appropriate system to showcase your work and a user-friendly container to transport it. If the quality of the finished portfolio could make potential employers envious, then your investment would be worthwhile. As you plan your book, consider "hiring" yourself as your own client. This strategy might inspire more probing and innovation during portfolio process.

Most young designers assemble their first portfolio from assignments given in design school. Typical problems consist of experimental visual exercises and case studies for theoretical clients. Other potential pieces come from student design competitions and free-lance work for actual clients. By graduation, most design students create a rather large body of work, which must be reduced to its essence by a thorough audit.

Some students feel "locked in" to selecting portfolio pieces strictly from school assignments. Coursework in strong design curriculums is intended to help develop critical thinking, visual literacy and creative methodology. The "products" or visual solutions reflect this process but may not necessarily produce a portfolio-quality piece on your initial attempt.

Prepare to revise all of your work that has "portfolio potential." Do not be satisfied to simply include a piece in your book just because it is clean, neat and received a passing grade. Your design sensitivity grows exponentially. Work that seemed strong a year or two ago might appear primitive now. If you remain open to revising, remodeling and refining your work, course assignments can provide the foundation of your creative portfolio.

Another effective approach involves creating all new pieces for your book, based on the assumption that your latest work is your best work. For example, if you designed a cultural poster for a class assignment, design a similar poster for an event involving your special interest and expertise. Build upon your previous course experience to create a superior portfolio piece. Perhaps extend the visual theme of the poster to invitations, ads and programs. This approach insures that your most sophisticated design effort is applied to problems which you have already experienced and have previously received feedback.

Impressive portfolio samples might emerge from "problem seeking" activities. Identify cultural groups, social organizations, environmental issues and political situations of particular personal interest. Or probe technology publications to anticipate products about to emerge in genetics, medicine or biomechanics. By creating visual solutions to high profile problems in society, your portfolio can reflect a personal perspective and provide graphic answers to "What if?"

---

**The work in your portfolio should: exhibit new ideas and concepts about communication, develop your point of view, provide clear solutions to complex problems in unique well crafted forms. Think of the portfolio as a filmstrip; this allows for placement and transition to be a dynamic part of the portfolio.**
Roger E. Baer
Associate Professor
Area Head, Graphic Design
College of Design
Iowa State University
Ames, IW

---

**Your portfolio is like your "brochure." The presentation is as important as the content. Design a presentation system that works for you. Don't just throw a bunch of mismatched pieces in a book.**
Randy Hipke
President
Hipke Freeman, Inc.
Glendale, CA

---

**You are your work. Only keep in your portfolio what you think represents you best. If you have to think twice about whether a certain piece should be included in your book it probably shouldn't. Fewer, better pieces will get the best response.**
Steve Stone
Founder/Creative Director
The Stone Group
San Francisco

**Do whatever you can to have printed pieces in your book. It shows someone believed in your work enough to pay to have it printed and helps set you apart from other student portfolios that only have assignments.**
David Carson
Art Director
David Carson Design
Del Mar, CA

---

**Avoid including work in your portfolio simply because it is printed. Often, students feel printed items have more credibility than school assignments. A poorly designed piece well printed is still poorly designed—this reflects on your ability to know the difference.**
Melissa Matlock
Adjunct Professor/
Graphic Design
California College
of Arts & Crafts
Oakland, CA

Redesign provides an additional opportunity to develop portfolio samples. Drawing from your design background, select a high profile corporation or institution. Completely redesign, on your terms, the visual identity, annual report, vehicle graphics, sample packages and important publications of the organization. Your entire portfolio will reflect one voice and demonstrate how you propose to upgrade an existing visual system. Show "before and after" samples for maximum impact.

Pieces produced *pro bono*, and those from co-op or internship experiences might earn a spot in your portfolio. You need a cold eye here. Many of these situations generate printed samples of inferior quality due to tight budgets, indifferent creative standards and average design direction. Because a piece has been funded and printed by a client does not guarantee its inclusion in your book. However, if it is exceptional and also printed, the piece will have powerful impact. Rely on your special mentor for feedback to help place your printed samples in perspective.

Design for the future is another direction you might elect to explore for your book. Project each problem you solved in the classroom five or ten years forward into time. This approach will demand careful research into lifestyle, media and technology trends. By taking a futurist position your portfolio can stand well ahead of your competition.

# Portfolio Audit

Your creative portfolio should not be a collection of all the work you have ever produced, only your very finest solutions. While a printed piece might hold sentimental value, it could be useless or even detrimental in your portfolio. A piece that earned you a top grade in a course might be out of place or appear disconnected in your book.

How do you decide what work to include? Too many young designers go it alone with no advice, a very risky approach. Find a tough editor with high standards. Take advantage of your design professor or refer to a respected design professional in your city. Remember, a job is not on the line here; you are most concerned with useful feedback. Plan for an hour or more of intense constructive criticism.

Collect and organize all potential portfolio pieces for the audit. If possible, schedule your meeting in a room with abundant table space. Group your pieces in categories. Place your publications, packaging, advertising, trademarks and promotions in separate areas. Spread your work out so all pieces in each category may be viewed at the same time. Include relevant sketches, briefs, slides and research data. This simple preparation will help your audit flow smoothly. Your editor will be able to provide you with relevant comments and avoid the redundancy that comes from jumping back and forth between unrelated pieces.

Be sure to write down your editor's comments about each potential portfolio piece. Use the form provided in this book or create your own system, perhaps with file cards. If you rely only on your memory of critical points discussed by your editor, key concepts might be lost.

The portfolio audit should help reveal your strengths and weaknesses. This rigorous evaluation of your work from a neutral, critical eye will help launch your creative portfolio. Eventually your work will fit into four distinct groups. Stack One will contain pieces ready to show or those that require slight refinement. Stack Two will hold pieces that indicate strong concepts but require remodeling to make them portfolio-ready. Stack Three will be discards, pieces with no real portfolio potential. Stack Four should be reserved for your editor's suggestions for additional design problems and process sketches to fill holes or strengthen particular sections of your book.

No two designers will show the same portfolio contents nor should they. If you have strong comprehensives and some quality printed pieces, then sizing and mounting might be your primary task. If on the other hand your samples are uneven with lackluster craft, the portfolio process will prove more formidable. In any case a serious audit will suggest a direction and predict a personal timeline to begin your job search.

**Don't confuse a body of work (everything you've ever done) and a portfolio (a select grouping of images consistent in style or subject). Base your portfolio on each client's need for what you do.**
Maria Piscopo
Principal
Creative Services
Costa Mesa, CA

**Only your very best goes in your portfolio. Like your mother said, "Neatness counts!" Originality counts . . . 12 to 15 samples . . . have two portfolios. Good Luck.**
Jack George Tauss
Executive Vice President
Jerry Fields Associates
Design Recruiters
New York City

**Inconsistency always sets off red lights in my mind. If there are three terrific pieces in a portfolio, three so-so ones, and three clunkers, which is the real you? And why can't you tell the difference? Do the terrific ones represent your teachers, bosses or colleagues more than you?**
Ellen Shapiro
President
Shapiro Design Associates
New York City

# Portfolio
# Audit Form

| | PORTFOLIO SAMPLE | PLATES | COMP. | COMMENTS/REVISIONS | IN PROGRESS | COMPLETE |
|---|---|---|---|---|---|---|
| 1 | | | | | | |
| 2 | | | | | | |
| 3 | | | | | | |
| 4 | | | | | | |
| 5 | | | | | | |
| 6 | | | | | | |
| 7 | | | | | | |
| 8 | | | | | | |
| 9 | | | | | | |
| 10 | | | | | | |
| 11 | | | | | | |
| 12 | | | | | | |
| 13 | | | | | | |
| 14 | | | | | | |
| 15 | | | | | | |
| 16 | | | | | | |
| 17 | | | | | | |
| 18 | | | | | | |
| 19 | | | | | | |
| 20 | | | | | | |

| | | | |
|---|---|---|---|
| SKETCHBOOK | | | |
| SKILLS BOOK | | | |
| PORTFOLIO CASE | | | |
| RESUME | | | |

# How Many Pieces?

Most successful creative portfolios contain between 10 and 20 pieces of work. This "optimum" refers to the number of problems presented, not a total number of boards or pages. Complex corporate identities, publications or sign systems often require several presentation boards or pages to communicate a clear problem solution.

Few designers can express both breadth and depth in 10 or fewer pieces. Showing more than 20 pieces usually reveals a creative weakness, poor editing or redundancy. By presenting too many samples, you risk infringing on the precious time of your reviewer. Excessive portfolio pieces leave the impression that you are uncomfortable prioritizing your work . . . or even worse that you are incapable of selecting effective design solutions. The idea of presenting a large number of design pieces with the idea that your reviewers will sort out their favorite things is a serious mistake.

Aim for 12 to 15 solid pieces. Prepare two or three additional high-quality solutions for reserve. Rotate these in and out of your presentation according to the focus of your interview target. Be prepared to develop replacement pieces if your interview process reveals critical gaps in your book. Keep your portfolio flexible. Make it adjustable to target specific employers and clients.

**You're only as good as your worst piece. If you have work you might make excuses about, leave it out! You want to communicate why you're satisfied with a project—how it solved the problem—how you learned something new.**
Karen SG Milnes
Art Director
Computer Curriculum
Corporation
Sunnyvale, CA

**Your portfolio is as strong as your weakest piece. The quality of imagination and craft should be primary, quantity secondary. Your work should provide evidence of style and personality.**
Larry Johnson
Professor of Art
CSU, Fullerton
Fullerton, CA

**A great advertising portfolio . . . not too much, just the best pieces with at least three campaigns. Solve problems conceptually, not just visually. Your portfolio should reflect the art director's/writer's ability to think, represent personality, and distinguish individuality.**
Thomas Saputo
V.P. Design Director
Team One Advertising
Los Angeles

# Portfolio
# Unity

**Show only your best work. Resist the temptation to show everything in the hope that something will strike just the right chord. Keep the quality of your portfolio uniform, whether you present three pieces or twenty three.**

Bunny Carter
Associate Chair for Design
San Jose State University
San Jose, CA

**Start with your best work first. Take out all personal work—fine art painting, cartoons and sculpture. Sketches that lead to final design solutions should be kept in a separate folder. Remember, the design of your portfolio presentation and resume is an extension of yourself and your design ability.**

Cheryl Roshak
President
Cheryl Roshak & Co.
Design Recruitment
New York City

**Your portfolio is only as strong as the worst piece in it. If a solution is questionable in concept or execution it should be eliminated because it sheds a bad light on the rest of the work in the portfolio.**

Lanny B. Sommese
Professor/Designer
Penn State University
State College, PA

Young designers often make the mistake of diluting the impact of their portfolios by including irrelevant pieces. The effective graphic design portfolio must demonstrate a careful focus and unity.

Omit all photographs, illustrations, paintings, drawings, renderings and fine art prints that stand alone as creative pieces. No matter how brilliant this work might be, art pieces differ from graphic design and will either compete with it or reduce the total impact of your portfolio.

The issue is intent. A fundamental difference exists between graphic design and fine art. The artist defines a problem for oneself and develops a personal visual solution. Graphic designers, working alone or collaborating with a design team, resolve clients' problems. They create alternative visual solutions that communicate to the client's selected audience. Graphic designers are hired to solve visual problems . . . not to make expressive personal art.

One proven approach is to demonstrate exceptional illustration, photography and rendering skills within the graphic design portfolio. Integrate your refined art techniques into your design solutions. Use a distinctive photo on a book cover or magazine spread. Show your unique illustration style on a poster or package. Demonstrate marker indication skills on a print ad or storyboard. Indicate your unique letterforms on a calendar, certificate or promotional apparel. Visual integration helps you show off your image-making ability in the context of your creative portfolio.

Another approach is to build a second but separate portfolio for illustration or photography. While the specifics of assembling these portfolios are beyond the scope of this book, the basic principles of the graphic design portfolio apply. Your reviewers will expect the same impeccable and intelligent presentation. However, your sample photographs and illustrations can stand as individual pieces rather than as applied samples.

Portfolio protocol permits you to show a second book during the interview. It is preferable to have a separate case for your photo or illustration portfolio. If you must use a single case, be sure to make a distinct visual transition between portfolios. Try a neutral board, color board or typographic board to divide the two books. Another approach is to mount your graphic design portfolio on black plates and your photo portfolio on archival white plates.

During the interview, first show your graphic design portfolio. Then with permission, show your secondary portfolio. Your interviewer will have the opportunity to view your creativity in greater depth. At best, the second portfolio can improve your perceived value. On the other hand, if the "other portfolio" is weak, it may cost you a target position.

# Format
# Size

Selecting the appropriate format size for your creative portfolio is critical. The portfolio audit will probably provide some good clues to formatting. Use the feedback from your audit to help bring a logical order to the many sizes, shapes, media and materials explored in your design coursework. Identify any visual threads that can create relationships between the samples deemed worthy of including in your book.

The ultimate goal is to integrate your best work into a unified presentation system. Strive for a single format size to show your samples—the advantages are many. One size will help interviewers focus on the quality of your work, not the presentation plates. This approach will make your book easier to handle, store and present during reviews. It will almost certainly help minimize your material purchases.

If you must deviate from the single-size format, do it with a purpose. Perhaps create a system with both full-size and half-size plates. Beware of the random format of haphazard sizes and shapes. You risk sending a message to interviewers that you lack organizational ability and do not really understand the visual "systems approach" on which much of graphic design is based.

A miniature format may crowd your work by reducing comfortable viewing grounds. Very large formats waste material, require more expensive cases and can be physically difficult to transport. Trying to show your huge portfolio in a cramped studio environment might prove to be a genuine nightmare.

What is "big enough but not too big?" This depends on the work you select for your book. One approach is to build your portfolio around the largest piece. For example if your largest piece is an 18"×24" printed poster, let this determine the format size. Smaller publications, collateral, and transparencies will easily fit. However if your largest piece is a 24×35 poster this choice would dictate an oversize format. Instead, select a more comfortable 16×20 format and include the poster as a 4×5 transparency.

If your portfolio has a publication focus, consider a format which effectively features the dominant 11×17 spread size. This may be accommodated on a 16×22 format with comfortable 2-1/2" borders. Or consider a borderless 11×17 bleed format. Another possibility is to insert folding publications or spreads into pockets on a portfolio plate, encouraging reviewers to handle your work as they would browse through a magazine or annual report.

A wise approach might involve sizing your portfolio to standard printed pieces produced during an internship or work developed in a series during your courses. If you plan to include five related 17×22 posters, adopt that size for your entire book. Try the 11×14 portfolio dimension if the bulk of your work is sized at 8 1/2×11 or 9×12.

**Design your portfolio much the same as you would a package or an annual report. Your objectives may include: flexible format, ease of use, appropriate size, lightweight. Focus on the work, not the portfolio. Keep it simple, not overbearing or overdesigned.**
Michael Osborne
President
Michael Osborne Design
San Francisco

| ATTACHE CASE SIZES |
| --- |
| 9 × 11 |
| 11 × 14 |
| 12 × 15 |
| 16 × 20 |
| 17 × 22 |
| 20 × 26 |

| CLAMSHELL BOX SIZES |
| --- |
| 8 × 10 |
| 11 × 14 |
| 14 × 17 |
| 16 × 20 |
|  |
|  |

| ZIPPERED CASE SIZES |
| --- |
| 9 × 11 |
| 11 × 14 |
| 14 × 18 |
| 16 × 20 |
| 17 × 22 |
| 18 × 24 |

| SHIPPING CASE SIZES |
| --- |
| 8 × 10 |
| 11 × 14 |
| 16 × 20 |
| 20 × 24 |
| 24 × 30 |
| 32 × 40 |

| PLATE BOARD SIZES |
| --- |
| 8 × 10 |
| 11 × 14 |
| 14 × 18 |
| 16 × 20 |
| 20 × 30 |
| 32 × 40 |

| COVER PAPER SIZES |
| --- |
| 19 × 25 |
| 20 × 26 |
| 23 × 35 |
| 25 × 38 |
| 26 × 40 |
| 38 × 50 |

| VIEW MAT SIZES | |
| --- | --- |
| 8.5 × 11 | TRANSP. |
| 11 × 14 | TRANSP. |
| 11.5 × 15.5 | TRANSP. |
| 12 × 16 | TRANSP. |
| 14 × 17 | TV |
| 19 × 24 | TV |

If your portfolio features three-dimensional graphics including packages, signage and exhibits, the all-transparency portfolio might be appropriate. Single 4×5 transparencies fit easily on standard 8×10 plates while the same size transparencies may be mounted two-up on 11×14 or 16×20 plates. Transparency portfolios are expensive to produce but easy to package.

An advertising portfolio should anticipate both single-page and spread ads for small page format *TV Guide*, standard page format *Newsweek*, and tabloid format *Interview*. If your format will comfortably show the 11×15 tabloid size, smaller formats will also fit. Television storyboard mats at 14×17 (4 panel) or 19×24 (8 panel) should be factored into your planning. Interpreting these dimensions might guide you to select an accommodating 19×24 format.

A limited budget might suggest a format size derived from standard 32×40 parent size illustration boards. Four 16×20 or two 20×32 boards will trim from the larger sheet with no waste. Take care here however, because forcing your creative portfolio into these expedient dimensions might prove a false economy.

Standard case dimensions and presentation material dimensions offer a good benchmark for determining your portfolio size. The comparison charts on this page provide a quick overview of relevant measurements. Generally speaking, a wider variety of cases are available to contain the smaller formats and prices tend to be lower for smaller portfolio cases.

# Portfolio
# Color

Color is a concern when selecting viewing grounds for your portfolio pieces. You need to pick a mounting color that will support your creative work but not visually dominate it. Beware of brightly colored pages or boards. Hues present in your creative pieces will be influenced by the color of your presentation mounts. For example, yellow background plates might lend a green cast to the process color in a brochure mock-up. Warm red presentation boards might pull the green saturation out of a publication spread and dilute its power. If the colors in your work optically shift, the impact of your portfolio will be compromised.

Black, gray and white give the most reliable presentation environments. These selections provide neutral viewing surfaces. Black survives handling, hides fingerprints and adds drama. White grounds work well for dark pieces but tend to show the wear of handling. White is less effective for showing ads and publications printed on white stock, as edges of the work tend to disappear.

Gray offers an alternative that deserves consideration. Less stark than black or white, grays are even more neutral. Warm grays feel "friendly" but may slightly affect colors in your samples. Cool grays are more "clinical" and stand away from your work. Medium or dark television grays work best for portfolio presentations.

Another alternative for portfolios is the ivory color acid-free archival board favored by photographers and museums. The natural color feels valuable and authentic, particularly if you use a French mat. Some of the pastel tans, golds and beiges have portfolio potential, as do the very dark umbers and sienna browns. Marbled and granite textured boards offer a "bookbinding" appearance.

Edges are a concern if you use illustration board for portfolio plates. The gray and black boards manufactured with identical surfaces and centers, Letramax SuperBlack® and 50-50 Total Gray® allow you to cut or bevel without a color change on the edges.

Portfolio color considerations should also extend to the backs of your plates or pages. When your book is being reviewed, pieces are often turned face down. Cover the board backs to add finish and surprise to your presentation. Consider adhering bright cast-coated paper to the backs of your black portfolio plates. Try bonding black cover stock or silver foil papers to the rear of your gray boards. Experiment with a change of color and surface on your portfolio plates. The result may favorably impress an employer by showing your careful attention to detail.

To insure the color consistency of your portfolio boards and cover papers, buy them in bulk from one source. Paper products tend toward slight color variations—one batch may vary from the next. Be sure to stockpile extra sheets to allow for mounting miscues and future additions to your book.

**Think of the portfolio as a portable gallery space. A well-designed portfolio allows the viewer's attention to be focused on the work; not the portfolio. The portfolio needs to be well-crafted, simple in design and neutral in color.**
James W. McManus
Professor, Art
CSU, Chico
Chico, CA

white plate mount

gray plate mount

black plate mount

# Process
# Sketches

Creative portfolios assembled to help you get an internship or entry-level position should contain process sketches. Top design offices insist on excellent sketching as a prerequisite for the collaborative process. Thumbnails, tissues, roughs and dummies help document your unique problem-solving approach. They demonstrate drawing skills, type indication techniques and color sensitivity. Process sketches both measure and chart your creativity. They show a design director your ability to generate abundant alternative solutions to a given problem.

Put yourself in the position of an employer facing a portfolio made up entirely of slick comprehensives and printed pieces. Certain questions arise. Were the solutions achieved alone or as part of a group project? How long did it take to produce the work? How will this designer communicate ideas in the studio environment? Without evidence of origin, are these derivative or original solutions? Where is the research behind each communication problem? Process sketches help answer all of these questions and give your reviewer a clear snapshot of your ability.

Showing too many sketches will certainly bore the creative director. Select three or four significant portfolio pieces to document. Sort your sketches to reflect the sequence of your solutions. It is not necessary to show every sketch. Include only those relevant sketches that mark key decision points in your process. Begin with a problem brief, continue with evidence of research and follow up with thumbnails, roughs and color studies.

Bind your process sketches with flexible covers to match your portfolio plates in color and finish. You might adhere them to backing pages to improve viewing. Or consider adopting a high quality, wire-bound sketchbook. Effective page sizes are 8 1/2"×11", 9×12 and 11×14. An alternative is to arrange loose sketches in a folded cover coordinated with your portfolio. This unbound system encourages handling and casual viewing but requires tidying up your sketches each time you show your work.

Do not crowd your sketches. Show the originals. Photocopies of idea sketches seem artificial and are less persuasive. Notations on the sketches should remain, as they help the reviewer track your process. Remove any grades or evaluation comments. Use tasteful divider sheets between each distinct problem. End papers will add a comfortable transition to your document. When complete, the sketchbook should invite handling, with pages that turn smoothly and binding that demonstrates your personal sense of craft.

Store the process sketchbook in the back of your portfolio case. Present it after showing your comprehensives and printed pieces to demonstrate how you work. An alternative is to call attention to your sketches after each documented problem. Weaving your sketchbook into the portfolio presentation shows the importance you attach to the design process. This approach can alter the rhythm of the review by inviting the tactile participation of your reviewer. Few designers can resist thumbing through a handsome sketchbook. Process sketches take advantage of this natural curiosity to add value and depth to your presentation.

**It is crucial to include process sketches to show how you think and develop an idea. Process sketches can be very revealing. For a strong designer, sketches will only enhance the portfolio and chances for a job.**
William Longhauser
Principal
William Longhauser Design
Philadelphia

**Have completely detailed thought processes of your work placed into separate project binders; at least for the major projects. Incorporate "real life" design solutions marketed towards the general consumer, if you do not have co-op experience. Present your portfolio with enthusiasm, explain your projects and maintain eye contact.**
Julie Stone
Vice President
Stone & Company,
Design Search Specialists
Braintree, MA

**Whether you are a professional or a student, present your most recent work with strong concepts. Whether the work has been produced or not, your ideas and thinking process are valuable assets to show.**
Piper Murakami
Designer
Pentagram Design
San Francisco

# Portfolio System

**The portfolio sounds like a lot of work. It's not. It's actually a lot of fun. You get to program, design and execute a complex system of integrated materials. That ought to be _fun_. It's what you've always claimed you _wanted_ to do, isn't it? So do it.**

Harry Murphy
Principal
Harry Murphy + Friends
Fairfax, CA

Harry Murphy, a prominent San Francisco graphic designer advises young designers to consider their portfolio as the key component of a total self-marketing system. In his eloquent and provocative presentations involving professional practice, Murphy encourages a serious global view of the portfolio process. He challenges designers to mount an all-out effort to take full advantage of the portfolio opportunity.

"It's job-hunting time, and time to assemble a 'portfolio'." So you go to Flax and buy one of those large black, multi-ring binders with the acetate sleeves (the ones that are aptly named "binders," and always bind and stick when anyone tries to turn the pages).

You gather up your various project assignments from school (the ones with the bent corners, missing pieces, coffee rings, cat pee stains, greasy fingerprints and an occasional stray nose booger). You pop these "representative samples" into the binder sleeves, and you're ready.

Right. You're ready for disappointment. You're ready to blame your job-hunting failure on "the economy." And eventually, you're ready to settle for a job serving cocktails, or driving a cab, or maybe clerking in your uncle's hardware store. Because you haven't created a portfolio at all. You've avoided the problem altogether. Worse yet, it appears you don't even _see_ the problem.

If you look closely, this "portfolio" thing actually is an _opportunity._ It's an opportunity (maybe one of your first) to design a comprehensive, integrated system of interviewing and presentation materials. And you _need_ to do it.

Your solution to this design problem should start with a broad overview, with the design of an _identity_ for yourself. This identity then can be applied in a consistent manner to the entire system. You'll need to design a coordinated letterhead, envelope and card, (for pre-interview communicating). And you'll need a resume, which should include samples of your best work (and maybe even your photograph). You ought to look at designing and building (or having built) a custom portfolio container or enclosure. Then you'll need to design and prepare a unified presentation system for your samples. All boards the same size and color. All titles the same, etc. And your presentation techniques need to be flawless. Seamless. Perfect. No kidding. No nicks, dings or hickeys. If there's a flaw and _you_ can see it, your _interviewer_ can see it. So fix it.

And finally you'll need to design some sort of mail-back, stay-in-touch piece to remind the interviewer that you still exist. (The _real_ job opportunity may come several months after your actual face-to-face interview.)

And when you've completed designing this integrated system of presentation materials, something unusual happens. It turns out that the system _is_ a portfolio. The medium has become the message. And you've demonstrated a high level of design skills. Conclusively.

Now here's the punch line. Pay attention. This elegant, beautiful, thoughtful, integrated, cohesive system _probably doesn't need any samples in it._ They can be blank pieces of paper, and you'd still get hired.

It's "Nike time." Just do it."

# Portfolio Sequence

Careful consideration should be given to determining your portfolio sequence. Put yourself in the chair of your interviewer. What order of presentation might be most logical, most impressive or most surprising? Will a particular sequence leave a positive lasting impression or create confusion? Will you be remembered by your strongest samples or by a less-important supporting piece? Can your ideal sequence communicate more quickly and conserve precious interview time?

One strategy involves showing your work beginning with simple pieces and finishing with complex problems. You might lead off with a trademark and finish with a publication redesign. Or your first piece could be a black and white newspaper ad with successive showings leading up to a comprehensive, integrated multi-media campaign.

Another approach is to think of your portfolio as a musical score. You create a sequence that has a modulated flow built around your strongest pieces. Like music, your portfolio can unfold with a dramatic opening, establish a compelling melody and lead to a powerful conclusion.

The knockout arrangement involves beginning your presentation with three powerful pieces. After being hit with a quick succession of explosive communication, the reviewer is won over. The remainder of your portfolio receives only a quick, cursory examination until the last piece which is also selected for its visual impact.

A proven sequence involves your three strongest pieces, placing one at the beginning, one in the middle and one at the end of your presentation. This concept involves making a strong initial impression, reinforcing that impression, then leaving your reviewer with your best impression. This approach is also effective if a reviewer thumbs through a book portfolio from back to front. Your three power pieces should be significant. Each might have won an award, been published or received other recognition worthy of extended discussion with your reviewer.

Jerry Kuyper, Senior Vice President of Siegel & Gale, the prominent strategic design firm, advises young designers to "Remove your least effective piece. Your portfolio is like a chain, only as strong as the weakest link. Start strong and finish stronger."

First and last pieces are the most important in any portfolio sequence and deserve your special consideration. Test the impact of these bookend pieces on several reviewers before finalizing the order of your book. Mark Ulriksen, art director of San Francisco Focus Magazine recommends that you "Make sure the quality of your work is consistent. The one lesser quality piece in your book is apt to stand out more than you'll realize. Start and end with your very best pieces."

If you plan to show idea or skill sketches, fit them in carefully. Unmounted sketches or sketchbooks will alter the pace of your presentation. It is not necessary to supplement each portfolio sample with sketches. However showing the process behind important "power" samples adds rich texture to your presentation.

**Show only your best work. Don't show anything you feel you need to explain or apologize for. Open and close with your very best work. It's as important to end well as to begin well.**
Laura Lamar
Art Director
MAX
San Francisco

**Start with strong pieces and end with strong pieces. The middle can flush out breadth and depth of skills and experience. But if the middle seems weak leave it home. Twelve to fifteen pieces is enough.**
Don Weller
Founder
The Weller Institute
for the Cure of Design
Park City, UT

**When I first took my book around, I noticed that it often lay open on the last page. From then on I always put the piece there that best represented the kind of work I wanted to do.**
Carm Goode
Professor Art, Design
Loyola Marymont
University
Los Angeles

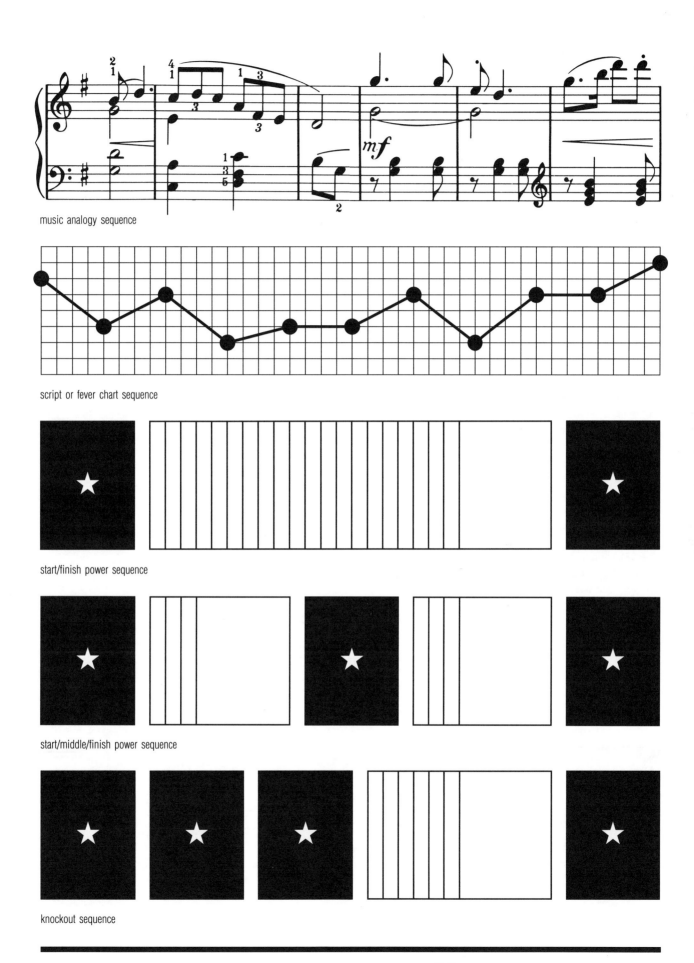

music analogy sequence

script or fever chart sequence

start/finish power sequence

start/middle/finish power sequence

knockout sequence

# Plate
# Portfolio

Plate portfolios display visual solutions on unbound pages, sheets or boards. The great advantage of a plate portfolio is that your presentation sequence is not locked in place. Modular plates allow you to arrange your sequence to fit a specific client or employer. This ability to customize your presentation is valuable if a series of interviews reveals a weak solution in your book. Replace the board with another sample or simply remove it. If feedback suggests a change in your order of presentation for greater impact, merely rearrange your boards.

Most plate portfolios are assembled from medium-weight illustration boards. Reliable brands include Strathmore®, Crescent®, and Letramax®. Medium-weight boards start to add up in carrying weight when your portfolio reaches 20 pieces. Heavyweight illustration board is more costly, difficult to cut and nearly twice as heavy to transport.

Another possibility for the plate portfolio is foam board. Rigid, lightweight and warp-resistant, this material is available in a variety of colors. One drawback is the 3/16" thickness. A stack of these plates (5 per inch) grows quickly. Edges of the foam board are fragile but can be trimmed with vinyl adhesive tape. A deep case works best to transport the foam board portfolio. An alternative is to select a large dimension case and store your plates in twin parallel stacks.

Sheet aluminum (1/16" thick) can be used for durable portfolio plates. The material is rust proof, lightweight and very durable. Aluminum may be cut in sheet metal or sign shops to your portfolio size. The surface may be brushed, polished or painted. Aluminum plates are costly but might lend a tactile, high-tech flavor to your creative portfolio.

Sheet plastics also hold potential for portfolio plates. Acrylics (Plexiglas®) are available in transparent, semi-opaque and colored opaque finishes. Polycarbonates (Lexan®) have durable shatter proof surfaces as do fiber-reinforced polyesters (Fiberglass®). Both are available in many colors and surfaces. Plastic laminates (Formica®) come in a wide range of colors and patterns. Although finished on only one side, laminates may be backed with paper or foil to create unique and memorable portfolio plates.

Sheet plastics must be precisely sized with particular care to edges and corners. As with aluminum plates, impeccable craft is necessary. Unless you have experience working with these materials, have your plates cut by professionals.

**Think materials.**
**Think thoroughly.**
**Think decisively.**
Brian Collentine
Principal
AXO Design Studio
San Francisco

**Make sure that your work shows before your boards. Be knowledgeable of who you are showing your portfolio to. Research them first. Show your design process: brainstorming, sketching, refinements, and final concepts with variations.**
Gwen Amos
Professor, Graphic Design
CSU, Sacramento
Sacramento, CA

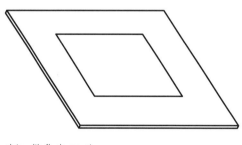

plate with flush mount

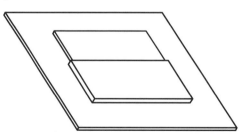

plate with pocket

plate with French mat

# Laminated Portfolio

Laminated plates are often used in creative portfolios. Both printed samples and flat mock-ups may be mounted on coverweight stock and laminated with transparent film. Ten mm polyester is most effective. Be sure to use a vendor who specializes in lamination and uses state-of-the-art equipment.

Both matte and gloss finishes are available. Lamination will enhance the color areas in your samples. It tends to brighten the surface and add depth. Be careful not to use wax adhesive or wax-base media if you decide to laminate. Heat applied to the transparent film during the coating process will cause bubbles to occur. Have your vendor laminate a sample plate before you trust your entire portfolio to this process.

Trim is critical when you select lamination. Plan on a 1/8" sealed border on each edge of your portfolio plate. This will increase the overall size of each piece. Flush trim of each plate is also possible, but yields more fragile edges and corners.

Laminated plates have some distinct advantages. Top-quality lamination adds years to the life of a portfolio piece. The tough, durable surfaces survive even the most careless handling. Your work becomes waterproof and scratch resistant. Finally, the weight of each plate is greatly reduced, as is the overall weight of your creative portfolio.

Beware of some disadvantages of lamination. It does not work well on thicker weights of illustration board. Because film is applied over your sample, the surface will reflect light. This effect may distract from your piece if you are simulating a soft uncoated paper surface. Also lamination will add several dollars cost per piece.

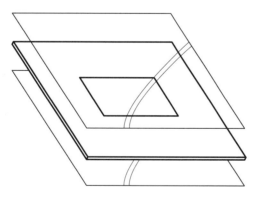

clear polyester seals portfolio plate

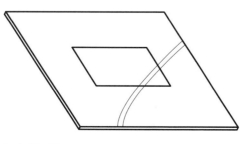

laminated plate

# Book Portfolio

Book portfolios incorporate binding systems to fasten and sequence pages. This type of portfolio presents your creative work in the form of a story from start to finish. One advantage of the book portfolio is that it "reads" in a familiar manner. Another is that it communicates without your presence in a drop-off situation. Book portfolios are more effective in smaller formats. Large pages seem awkward, are difficult to turn, and lack the friendly "feel" of a book.

Some common binders durable enough to hold portfolio pages are ring, toothed and screw-post systems. Ring binders have three or four rings as pivot points. Small-diameter rings are less obtrusive and most effective for thin flexible jackets. Large diameter rings are essential if your portfolio pages are drilled illustration board. Asymmetric slanted rings (D-rings) are more user-friendly than the common circular type and help pages lay flat.

Toothed binders are very strong but with so many pivots (on 1/2" centers) and holes to match, pages tend to hang up. These binders are most common in low-end portfolio books. Tooth systems are notorious for sticking or jamming during interviews. If you choose a toothed binder, make sure the teeth register perfectly.

Screw-post binders are foolproof and nearly invisible. This system securely anchors pages at two or three points. Pages are inserted or deleted with a screwdriver. Because the binding is so understated, full attention is focused on your work. With this system however, pages will not lay perfectly flat.

Binder inserts hold your creative work in the book portfolio. These transparent jackets trap and protect your work. Three types of jackets are available. Acetate sleeves are provided with most standard book portfolios. These work fine with thin samples. Consider replacing the standard, black paper backing with printed black or gray paper, spray-mounted to cover-weight stock. The thicker sheets will add heft and rigidity to your pages. Acetate covers will scratch with heavy use, are unstable and will stretch with changes in heat and humidity.

Polyester (Mylar®) jackets are preferable to acetate. Archival poly preserves and protects your work. It is a very stable material, will not bond to your design samples and has a durable, tear-resistant surface that will survive handling.

Clear, non-glare vinyl jackets offer a third alternative for the book portfolio. Vinyl is softer and more flexible than acetate or poly. It works well for printed portfolio samples. However, vinyl tends to cling to design mock-ups and may remove or disturb the surfaces of press type, color-comp or photocopy surfaces.

Page jackets are very cumbersome for showing brochures, booklets or publications. For maximum impact, multi-page pieces should be held and thumbed through. The repetitive act of removing and replacing work in page jackets slows the review process. Samples smaller than the portfolio page tend to slide around inside the jacket.

**Think of your portfolio as a "brochure" for yourself with each panel as a page or spread. Apply all the design discipline you would for any other client's project. Also, keep in mind that you will be judged by the worst piece that you feel is acceptable to include.**

Pierre Rademaker
Principal
Pierre Rademaker Design
San Luis Obispo, CA

An alternative is to create custom pages for the book portfolio. Surfaces that display your creative samples remain uncovered (and unprotected). Custom pages may be cut from medium-weight illustration board, thin sheet aluminum or 1/16" Plexiglass®. These materials, while rather thick for pages, have good rigidity. Binding holes must be drilled oversize to aid turning each page. Consider cutting tight radius corners on the outside edges of each page to facilitate handling.

Permanent binding systems offer limited potential for the book portfolio. Perfect binding is elegant and gives the rich tactile feel of a limited edition. Wire binding systems allow book pages to turn easily and lay completely flat. Spiral, comb and stitched binding systems are inexpensive but lack the quality connotation so important for the creative portfolio.

The format of the book portfolio sets up special viewing problems. Other than opening and closing pages, the book communicates in two-page spreads. If both pages exhibit work, be sure that your samples do not compete. An alternative is to show only on the right hand page of each spread. More pages are required but each piece speaks for itself. Avoid grouping unrelated small samples on pages of the book portfolio.

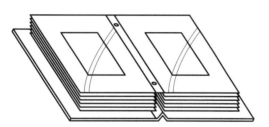

book with screwpost binding

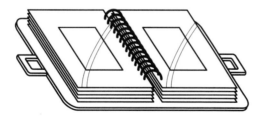

book with toothed ring binding

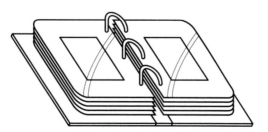

book with D-ring binding, radius corners

| BINDING FOR BOOK PORTFOLIOS | |
| --- | --- |
| ❶ PERFECT BINDING | $$$ |
| ❷ WIRE-O-BINDING | $$ |
| ❸ PLASTICOIL® BINDING | $ |
| ❹ VAL-O® BINDING | $ |
| ❺ PLASTIC COMB BINDING | $ |
| ❻ STRING/TIE BINDING | $ |
| ❼ SADDLE STITCH BINDING | $ |

# Easel
# Portfolio

Easel portfolios exhibit creative work to clients and employers in a comfortable, upright viewing position. Your case becomes a stand with your work on stage at the center of attention. Easel formats are widely used by sales professionals and are familiar to your interviewer. Cases for easel presentations are available in both stock and custom versions.

Easels work effectively with both plate systems and binding systems. Portfolio plates fit snugly into the clamshell box easel and may be displayed either one or two up. Binder portfolios are attached to easel cases with wire, ring or screwpost fastening systems.

Collapsible desktop easel stands are useful for displaying plate portfolios. These telescoping metal stands are small enough to be carried inside most portfolio cases. Your work is displayed at a proven viewing angle on non-skid feet or a base. Box cases may be modified to incorporate a folding easel with a hinged sheet of illustration board, metal or plastic.

One advantage of the easel portfolio is that you are in control of where you show your work. The desktop easel consumes very little space, no more than the area of your case. A portable easel requires even less table space. Easel presentations work best with both presenter and reviewer facing the portfolio. An easel helps you pace your presentation yet invites an employer to handle portfolio plates for closer inspection.

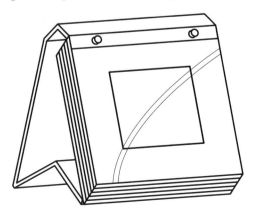

# Folder
# Portfolio

Folder portfolios offer a unique system
for showing creative work. A modular
folder similar to a file jacket is prepared
for each portfolio piece. If most of your
creative samples measure 8 1/2"×11",
the folder page dimensions might be
9×12. Each folder becomes a package
to be opened and examined. Some work
is mounted to the inside panels of the
folders. Brochures, publications, transparencies and sketches fit into pocket
versions of the folders.

Cover-weight stocks make good folder
materials. Make your own duplex sheets
by spray mounting together two cover-
weight sheets of distinct colors. The
inside of each folder should be black or
gray for effective viewing. Precision
cutting is necessary to ensure that each
folder matches the others. Carefully
score all fold lines before assembly. Add
a brief project title to the front cover of
each folder with press-type. This will help
orient the folders and identify their
sequence.

Folder portfolios work best when your
presentation includes 10 to 12 pieces.
Opening 20 or more folders will be tedi-
ous for your reviewer. A single stack of
folders becomes quite thick and requires
a deep case. Two side-by-side stacks will
fit most standard cases. The folder portfolio is excellent for protecting your
creative work because each sample is
under cover. This system requires consid-
erable handling. A careful choice of paper
colors will prolong folder life and hide
fingerprints.

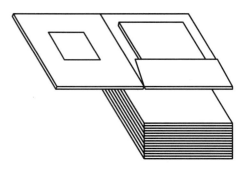

folder system with pocket insert

# Transparency Portfolio

Transparency portfolios are effective for showing three-dimensional models, packages, exhibits, vehicles and sign systems. Oversized posters, illustrations, outdoor advertising and point-of-purchase pieces lend themselves to transparencies as do promotional photographs that combine design applications. Trademark portfolios (symbols, logotypes, letterforms, calligraphy) also show well in transparency form.

Transparencies are not particularly effective for presenting the nuances of business systems, brochures, annual reports, magazine spreads, advertising and editorial illustration. The reduced size of transparencies alters the scale of type and perception of your reviewer. If your transparencies are projected as slides, type and images appear oversize. The subtle surface changes of varnish, foil, emboss and diecutting are difficult to detect on transparencies. Color is likely to shift a bit depending on film and photographic lighting. Follow this guideline . . . If the piece is intended to be hand-held and read close-up, avoid transparencies. If the image is designed to communicate at a distance or in three dimensions consider transparencies.

The most common transparency sizes are 35 mm, 2 1/4" square, 4×5 and 8×10. Inexpensive and easy to process, the universal 35 mm slides and 2 1/4 square sizes have limited potential for the transparency portfolio. Size is the problem. The film image is just too small to show detail without projection. Remember that your transparency portfolio will seldom be projected on first viewing, but examined directly on a light table or held up to available light.

Large 8×10 transparencies provide great clarity and if available should be considered for your portfolio. This expensive format is available only in larger markets. Request direct transparencies. Avoid those produced by the internegative enlargement process from 35 mm slides, as your images might soften. A disadvantage of the large format image is the great expense associated with studio and location shooting. Usually only custom color houses process 8×10 transparencies, adding to your portfolio costs. Also the large film size is more difficult to mount and protect from damage.

The 4×5 format offers the advantages of viewing size, economy and the availability of film and processing. While established studios and agencies might prefer the 8×10 size, most young designers will find 4×5 transparencies adequate for entry level portfolios. For best results photograph your work (or have it shot) directly with a 4×5 camera. Specify E-6 Ektachrome processing. An acceptable alternative is to provide 35 mm slides (E-6 processing) and have them converted to the 4×5 size through the internegative process by a quality custom color processing lab.

Transparency portfolios are best produced as a series of plates mounted for protection. Alternatives are the Savage Prevue Mount® and Light Impressions TransView® systems. Transparencies slip into precut black mounts that mask off edges of your film. These 10 1/2×13 1/2 board-weight plates hold twelve 35 mm slides, twelve 2 1/4 square transparencies or four 4×5 transparencies. One disadvantage is that multiple images on each plate might compete with each other. Four posters or four packages will form a natural cluster while the diversity of a trademark, a cover, a vehicle and a print ad shown together on a single plate will diminish the focus of your book. The smaller 8 1/2×11 and 11×14 mounts that show one or two transparencies offer greater flexibility in your portfolio sequence.

**Your transparency portfolio should achieve a simple, classic look that will last. The system should accommodate future additions with ease. It is most important that the work you select stands alone and is powerful in concept. My portfolio is a black 11×14" format which comfortably holds 2 1/4", 4×5", 5×7" and 8×10" transparencies. Each cover plate tastefully identifies my studio and becomes a quiet, miniature ad. Do not compromise the photo quality in your book—consult a professional. Be sure to show your work in a simple environment that doesn't take away from the work itself.**

Dan Escobar
Principal
Escobar Photography
San Francisco

A preferred technique is to mount each transparency individually or in pairs on window mats that you construct. Efficient sizes for single 4×5 transparency plates are 8×10, 8 1/2×11, and 9×12. Good sizes for double transparency plates are 9×12, 12×12 or 11×14. Double window plates are effective for showing alternative solutions, before/after redesign and design in application.

Transparencies are fragile and scratch easily. For maximum protection cover the front of each transparency with a layer of clear 3 mm polyester or acetate. Back the transparency with a thin sheet of frosted 3 mm Mylar® to diffuse light as your plate is held up for viewing. Tape the sandwich of transparency and films to the rear of the window in your portfolio plate with Magic® tape. Back the reverse side with cover weight paper (with a window the size of your transparency trimmed out). Spray mount the backing paper to the window plate to finish the piece.

Transparency portfolios have several advantages. The small plate size is easy to handle and transport. Quality transparencies give your work a jewel-like professional appearance. As a system they can be easily viewed in the office environment without projection. The color fidelity and sharpness of transparencies shows your work at its best. If your budget permits, give strong consideration to a transparency portfolio.

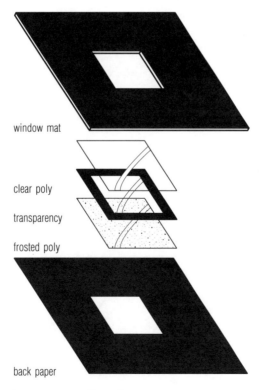

window mat

clear poly

transparency

frosted poly

back paper

transparency mounting system

window mats, TransView®, Savage Prevue®

# Color Print Portfolio

Color prints may be used to build your creative portfolio. As with transparencies, color prints are not effective for showing print pieces with intricate detail. Three-dimensional packages, models and interiors translate well. Although more expensive than transparencies, quality C-prints display your creative portfolio without the need for back lighting.

The most common process for producing color prints involves negative film. However, the automated labs that produce billions of prints annually are not a reliable source. For portfolio-quality color prints, try the same custom color labs used by professional photographers in your market. You will pay a premium, but each negative will be carefully printed to your satisfaction. Be a tough critic. Check carefully for adequate contrast, precise edges, color tonality, faithful cropping and flawless surface. If your prints don't measure up, have them redone.

The Cibachrome® system produces sharp, high quality color prints directly from slides or transparencies. Available in both matte or gloss finishes, these prints feature brilliant color fidelity but rather fragile surfaces that require careful handling. Cibachromes are more easily proofed than other C-prints, as you are comparing two positive images.

The common color print sizes are 4"×5", 5×7, 8×10, 11×14 and 14×17. The two smaller sizes might make your book resemble a photo album. The larger formats preferred by professional photographers create visual impact but are the most expensive and demand larger viewing grounds. Most graphic designers find that 8×10 color prints are affordable, communicate well when hand-held, and allow a smaller portfolio. Avoid combining two or more print sizes in your book.

Mat sizes for color prints should include a comfortable viewing border of at least two inches on the top and both sides, with a bit more on the bottom. Larger format prints can be effectively mounted full bleed without borders. Color prints communicate best on black or gray mats.

Consider protecting the surface of your color prints. The clear acetate or polyester pages in a book portfolio work well. Laminating a plate will add a protective invisible layer as will wrapping a photoboard with polyester. French mats help shield your photo surfaces from scratching. Although unwieldy in presentation, hinged covers or slip sheets of polyester or vellum will help protect your investment in color prints.

If you are seeking an entry-level position, show me examples of perfect production and your ability to work with type. All-transparency portfolios make it difficult to see craftsmanship and type refinement. Show me some real pieces—student comps can be a great way to indicate your level of craft and your understanding of type. For a junior designer position demonstrate your ability to handle all aspects of a project from design conception through printing supervision.
Melanie Doherty
Principal
Melanie Doherty Design
San Francisco

Our small studio demands flexible performance from each designer: identities, publications, promotions, illustration and even copywriting; all for budgets that range from handsome to non-existent. I look for portfolios that show ideas and execution across similar ranges.
Lila Wallrich
Principal
Wallrich and Landi Design
Sacramento, CA

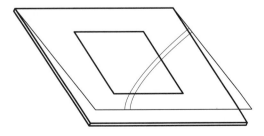

C-print with protective flap

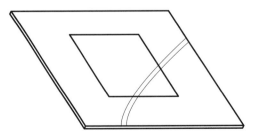

C-print with wrapped poly cover

# Electronic Portfolio

**The most important thing to have in an electronic portfolio is a clear concise interface which enables the viewer to see your work easily and on its own. Don't rely on whizzy effects or gratuitous animation. As always, keep it simple and elegant.**

Dale Horstman
Art Director
Electronic Arts, Inc.
San Mateo, CA

**Support your portfolio samples with laser prints of key work-in-progress stages. Include preliminary roughs through electronic mechanical layouts. Demonstrate to me your understanding of the correct processes by showing competence in planning and quality in execution.**

Hall Kelley
Principal
Hall Kelley Organization
Sunnyvale, CA

**When looking at your portfolio, I like to see how you solve a complicated communication problem. Trying to show me a shopping list of your skills is the wrong thing to do. A portfolio of a handful of well thought out ideas is better than a history of every project you've worked on.**

Clement Mok
Information Architect
Creative Director
Clement Mok Designs, Inc.
San Francisco

Many creative portfolios are now produced in electronic rather than print form. Interactive technology expert Dr. John Ittelson of California State University, Chico feels "the only limitations today are not the technology to produce and review the electronic portfolio but the designer's ability to be creative with these new tools." Ittelson continues, "interactive electronic photos, video and type that looks superb to the untrained eye, appears just fair to the graphic designer. As the technology systems standardize, they help encourage electronic portfolios." One example is the Kodak photo CD system which allows transparencies to be scanned at full resolution, manipulated and viewed on both television and computer screens. Another is the Internet with provides a huge international audience for your portfolio.

Hypermedia allows designers to merge text, drawings, photographs, animation, video and sound in an interactive format. Translated, this means your portfolio can include high resolution photo samples of your work called up in any order. Portfolio images can be embellished with typographic titles or brief statements supplemented by your own voice over a musical background. At strategic intervals a video of you explaining your work and design philosophy emerges to guide the sequence. The presentation might conclude with a review of your resume with type sized and color-coded to highlight your strengths.

An effective electronic presentation can demonstrate conceptual skills not common to most graphic designers who are used to thinking in terms of images frozen for print. Design for hypermedia involves a sensitivity to scripting, image sequence and viewer navigation. It can showcase your ability to organize according to hierarchies, matrices, series, overlays, spatial zooms, webs and parallel texts. The electronic portfolio can add dimension to your creativity and raise your perceived value by an employer.

Electronic portfolios have some potential drawbacks. Exceptional quality is essential. Commonplace productions will fail, as they will be measured against television commercials, video and films in the mass media. Extreme subtleties of print including varnish, fragile type and fine lines do not translate well to electronic displays.

Your portfolio must fit the playback hardware of the employer . . . a problem which might rule out some excellent opportunities. However technical advances of thin screen and high definition technology permit you to transport refined playback hardware in a lightweight laptop format. Perhaps the major problem is that the electronic portfolio takes you out of the human loop, unable to respond in person to the spontaneous questions of your reviewer.

One use of this exciting media is as a screening tool for employers and placement professionals. Designers are able to market themselves and their work worldwide without expensive travel. The number of in-person interviews are reduced as more complete information can be projected by the electronic portfolio. Finalists for a position will be interviewed in the traditional manner or by video telephone.

# Visionary Portfolio

The visionary portfolio defines its own standard. It reflects your unique stance and sets you far apart from your competition. A visionary solution usually starts from the position of "How far can I push my portfolio?" or "What is the essence of my portfolio?" Be prepared to break tradition. Explore new technologies, exotic materials and unusual formats. Probe the entire portfolio process. Can you eliminate, transfer, modify, simplify or combine its parts? Think big. Take some risks. The potential payoff from a visionary portfolio is enormous.

Your visionary portfolio may begin in several ways. Perhaps it will develop in a dream or during your morning shower. It may have roots in an exercise session or even while you enjoy a walk. This special portfolio may derive from unique insight, abstraction or transformation. However your visionary portfolio will probably result from the see/imagine/draw process that drives most design activity.

Performance criteria can help frame the scope of your visionary portfolio. Charles Eames, an American design genius stated in the film *Design Q & A,* "Here is one of the few effective keys to the design problem—the ability of the designer to recognize as many of the constraints as possible—his willingness and enthusiasm for working within these constraints—the constraints of price, of size, of strength, balance, of surface, of time, etc.; each problem has its own peculiar list."

Explore some of these performance parameters to stimulate your visionary portfolio. How *large* must it be? How *small* can it be? Should you carry it by a handle, under your arm, in a pocket or pull it behind you? Might you reduce weight through unusual materials or miniaturization? Can your visionary portfolio become its own package? Might you join your creative samples with an unusual connector, a special hinge, clip or sleeve? Will your portfolio travel well under an airplane seat? Can it easily clear customs if you decide to travel abroad? If you diligently explore the edges of the problem you might open the door to an innovative portfolio.

Compare your visionary portfolio to a fine automobile. The case should demonstrate a refined form, a flawless finish, functional hardware and tight tolerances. An inviting interior should delight the eye with tactile coverings, impeccable craft and fine detailing. Careful ergonomic planning allows the contents to be protected when stored, but easily removed when handled for inspection. Your presentation plates should display flawless surfaces, precise dimensions and an appropriate color system both front and back that adds value to your visual samples. In the words of the great architect Mies van der Rohe "God is in the details."

To achieve "quintessence," the very essence, heart and core of the visionary portfolio is difficult. Few are capable of total innovation, but you should consider the challenge. Examples of truly elegant solutions are the Porsche 911, Ray-Ban Sunglasses, the Swiss Army Knife, the Tizio Lamp and the Macintosh Power-Book. These products communicate immediately with both form and function. They achieve a visual elegance, with soul. If your visionary portfolio reveals its purpose, appears inevitable and inspires the comment "Aha!" or "That's it!", you are on your way.

I have always been impressed with students and professionals who approach their portfolio and presentation as a design problem, with solutions ranging from transparencies that fit into a matchbox to elaborate images on a CD or floppy disc. When it comes to hiring a designer, my final decision is always based on a review of your visual journals or sketches that illustrate a thorough design process.
Conrad Jorgensen
Principal
Conrad Jorgensen Studio
San Francisco

Always remember the essential rule in developing your portfolio is that there are no rules. Your samples have to demonstrate your past, present and future and be aware that your book is as strong as the weakest piece.
Roz Goldfarb
President
Roz Goldfarb Associates
Creative Connections
New York City

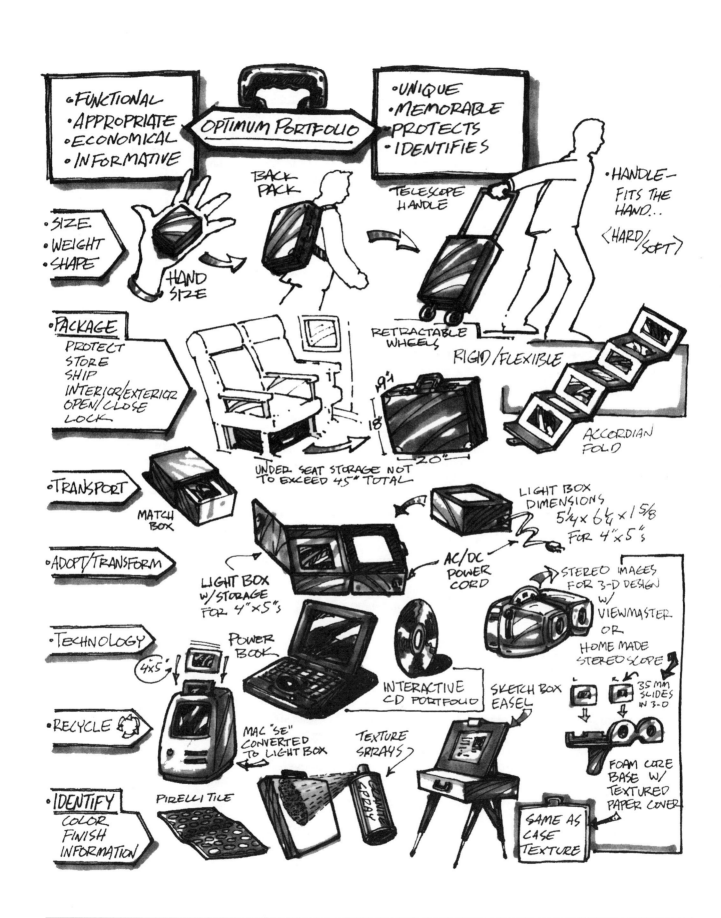

- FUNCTIONAL
- APPROPRIATE
- ECONOMICAL
- INFORMATIVE

OPTIMUM PORTFOLIO

- UNIQUE
- MEMORABLE
- PROTECTS
- IDENTIFIES

- SIZE
- WEIGHT
- SHAPE

BACK PACK

HAND SIZE

TELESCOPE HANDLE

- HANDLE—
FITS THE
HAND...
⟨HARD/SOFT⟩

- PACKAGE
PROTECT
STORE
SHIP
INTERIOR/EXTERIOR
OPEN/CLOSE
LOCK

RETRACTABLE WHEELS

RIGID/FLEXIBLE

19"

18"

20"

UNDER SEAT STORAGE NOT
TO EXCEED 45" TOTAL

ACCORDIAN FOLD

- TRANSPORT

MATCH BOX

LIGHT BOX
DIMENSIONS
5 1/4 x 6 1/4 x 1 5/8
FOR 4"x5"s

- ADOPT/TRANSFORM

LIGHT BOX
w/ STORAGE
FOR 4"x5"s

AC/DC
POWER
CORD

STEREO IMAGES
FOR 3-D DESIGN
w/
VIEWMASTER
OR
HOME MADE
STEREO SCOPE

- TECHNOLOGY

4"x5"

POWER BOOK

INTERACTIVE
CD PORTFOLIO

SKETCH BOX
EASEL

35 MM
SLIDES
IN 3-D

- RECYCLE

MAC "SE"
CONVERTED
TO LIGHT BOX

TEXTURE
SPRAYS

FOAM CORE
BASE W/
TEXTURED
PAPER COVER

- IDENTIFY
COLOR
FINISH
INFORMATION

PIRELLI TILE

SAME AS
CASE
TEXTURE

# Portfolio Cases

Portfolios are defined as flat portable cases used to carry documents, manuscripts and drawings. The container for your creative portfolio houses, protects and stores precious concepts and samples. It serves as a repository of your best ideas. A portfolio case, intelligently selected or constructed will last throughout your design career.

Your case makes a professional statement, even before opening it to show your samples. Case color, finish and details help define your professional stance. Case selection is an important design decision and will be inspected with the same scrutiny as your portfolio contents and attire. A unique case can help raise the professional perception of your work.

The event of opening your case provides a rich opportunity to add drama to the interview. Remember your childhood experiences of opening a package on your birthday or Christmas. Even the most wizened employer, client or placement professional can be moved by that first glance inside your case. Seize the moment by presenting an unusual color or tactile material that begs to be touched.

The sound of opening your portfolio case demands attention. Do the locks snap open with a startling crack, or do they purr open like the doors of a Mercedes? Perhaps lube your case hardware to soften the sound. Consider installing a tasteful sound chip to announce each opening with a few appropriate musical notes, a strategy which may pay dividends if you decide to drop off your book. Stimulating the aural sense of interviewers can help make your portfolio more memorable.

Manufactured cases are available in a wide assortment of styles and sizes. Shop carefully for your case. Take the time to inspect hardware, corners, storage pockets and finish. Make sure the case is not too heavy, as it will gain the additional weight of your book. Measure the *interior* dimensions before you buy. If you have sufficient lead time make your purchase during January or summer when most art suppliers conduct sales events. Mail order involves a bit more risk and demands prudence in your search for the most appropriate portfolio case. Reliable sources for high quality cases are listed on page 76.

If you select a manufactured case for a plate portfolio, interior dimensions will certainly be larger than plate dimensions. Construct a filler insert to shim the remaining space. The filler should firmly hold portfolio plates to avoid the sliding and rubbing motion that will gradually damage surfaces and edges. Case fillers can be crafted of high density foam, illustration board, wood, plastic, styrofoam or rubber. Be sure to plan for a finger slot or thin strap to ease removing your plates. A beautiful case with sloppily crafted fillers will disappoint your reviewer. Devise a case insert that enhances the handling of your creative work and stimulates interest at the moment of opening.

One accessory that should be seriously considered for transporting your portfolio case is a shoulder strap. This simple device can be a real energy saver if you have a long walk to an interview. The shoulder strap helps distribute the weight of your case and may be disconnected for a portfolio drop-off. Another transport possibility is to adapt the handy luggage wheels or portable carts used by frequent travelers and airline crews.

**The carrying case for your portfolio can be a design statement unto itself. Choose one that will accommodate the size and shape of your presentation boards or format the boards to fit the case. Consider making it yourself or having one custom made.**
Doug Akagi
Principal
Akagi Design
San Francisco

**The portfolio package can transcend basic function by becoming itself a thoughtful design solution. Innovative use of materials, impeccable craft, and well-written project descriptions can help make your portfolio system truly exceptional.**
Michael Shea
Senior Designer
Jager, DiPaola, Kemp
Burlington, VT

**ATTACHE BOX** CUSTOM CASE CO.

**TRANS-PORT BAG** LIGHT IMPRESSIONS

**LIPPED CLAMSHELL BOX** LIGHT IMPRESSIONS

**TRANS-PORT SHIPPER** LIGHT IMPRESSIONS

**TRIMLINE ATTACHE BOX** FLAX

**ZIPPERED BOOK** FABER-CASTELL

**ARCHIVAL ALBUM** LIGHT IMPRESSIONS

**EASEL BOOK** BREWER-CANTELMO

**EASEL BOX** BREWER-CANTELMO

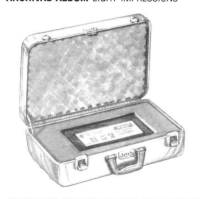

**ALUMINUM BRIEFCASE** ZERO HALLIBURTON

**ALUMINUM CARRY BOX** FLAX

**LIGHT BOX PORTFOLIO** CUSTOM MADE

# Presentation
# Comprehensives

| Portfolio Subject | Comprehensive Techniques | Considerations |
|---|---|---|
| Trademark Symbol Logotype Lettermark | PMT positive (black image) | Adjust the apparent size of each mark so that all have equal visual weight. Size the marks to a three inch maximum dimension. Presenting your marks in color adds impact and meaning. |
| | PMT negative (white image) | |
| | Film negative, color behind | |
| | Custom transfer (Chromatech®, Identicolor®) | |
| | Laser print, RC, film output | |
| | Color printout (laser, dye transfer) | |
| Letterforms Calligraphy | Original (ink, paint, airbrush) | Consider showing these in application, as part of your cover, ad, poster, promotion or editorial layout. |
| | Color transparency | |
| | Color printout | |
| Typography Experimental Forms Calendar Title Page Infographic Certificate Specimen Page | PMT, positive, negative | Show your typographic insight and sensitivity by designing within the limits of type and color. Select processes that reflect your precision and control. |
| | Transfer type | |
| | INT® (3M process) | |
| | Omnicrom® on photocopy | |
| | Color Tag® on photocopy | |
| | Laser print/RC, film output | |
| | Custom transfer | |
| | Color printout | |
| Poster | Original (ink, paint, airbrush) | Show originals or printed posters to add impact and color to your book. Posters larger than your portfolio format may be shown with transparencies. |
| | Screen print | |
| | PMT positive, negative | |
| | Film positive, negative, color behind | |
| | Bubble Jet® color photocopy | |
| | Color transparency | |
| | Color printout | |

| Portfolio Subject | Comprehensive Techniques | Considerations |
|---|---|---|
| Newspaper Ad<br>Magazine Ad<br>Yellow Pages Ad<br>Direct Mail | Tear sheet (printed ad)<br>Marker indication (color)<br>PMT positive, negative<br>Velox (from negative)<br>Film negative, color behind<br>Laser print/RC, film output<br>Color printout | Show all ads full size. By presenting a series of ads you can demonstrate format and type system. Write all headlines and body copy to showcase your verbal capabilities. |
| Book Cover<br>Magazine Cover<br>CD, Cassette Cover<br>Report Cover | Marker indication<br>PMT positive, negative<br>Film negative, color behind<br>Color printout | This is an opportunity to integrate your original photograph, illustration and fine art into cover samples. |
| Newspaper<br>Newsletter | Tear sheet<br>PMT positive<br>Velox (from negative)<br>Laser print/RC output<br>Color printout | Present front page, editorial page, section pages, financial page and infographics at full-size or half-size. Newsletters can be mounted in a pocket to encourage handling. |
| Magazine<br><br>Consumer<br>Trade<br>Corporate<br>Journal<br>Experimental | PMT positive, negative<br>Color photocopy<br>Custom transfer<br>Laser print/RC, film output<br>Color printout | Show cover alternatives, table of contents, feature spreads and department sections. Present at full-size or half-size with original photos and illustrations. |

# Presentation
# Comprehensives

| Portfolio Subject | Comprehensive Techniques | Considerations |
|---|---|---|
| Annual Report<br>Quarterly Report<br>Identity Manual<br>Sales Manual | PMT positive, negative<br><br>Color photocopy<br><br>Custom transfer<br><br>Laser print, RC, film output<br><br>Color printout | Show cover, editorial spreads, contents, financials: Integrate original illustration, photography and infographics. Present at full-size, half-size or quarter-size to indicate systems design. |
| Brochure<br>Folder<br>Press Kit<br>Paper Promotion<br>Self Promotion<br>Invitation<br>Greeting Card | Printed piece<br><br>PMT positive, negative<br><br>Omnicrom®, Color Foil® on photocopy<br><br>Color Tag® on photocopy<br><br>Laser print, RC output<br><br>Color printout | Present as folding mock-ups in portfolio plate pocket to show reading sequence. Invite reviewer to handle and examine these pieces. |
| Business System<br><br>Letterhead<br>Envelope<br>Business Card<br>Business Forms | PMT positive<br><br>Omnicrom®, Color Foil® on photocopy<br><br>Color Tag® on photocopy<br><br>Custom transfer<br><br>Laser print, paper output<br><br>Color printout | Present with strategic, signed letter. Address and stamp envelope to indicate how the system functions in use. |

| Portfolio Subject | Comprehensive Techniques | Considerations |
|---|---|---|
| Sign<br>Sign System<br>Directory<br>Transit Map<br>Vehicle Identity<br>Exhibit<br>Retail Space<br>Outdoor Advertising<br>Transit Board | Marker indication<br><br>Blueprint, blackline, sepia print<br><br>PMT positive, negative<br><br>Custom transfer<br><br>Laser print, RC, film output<br><br>Color transparency<br><br>Custom C-print<br><br>Cibachrome® print<br><br>Color printout | Elevations or perspective renderings complete with scale figures offer one alternative. Transparencies of the renderings are another. Preferred are high quality color transparencies or C-prints of 3-dimensional models complete with scale human figures. |
| Apparel<br><br>Uniform<br>T-Shirt<br>Cap<br>Hard Hat | Color printout<br><br>Marker indication<br><br>Color transparency<br><br>Cibachrome® print | Color rendering on scale model is adequate. Best are transparencies or color prints of human models wearing attire. |
| Packages<br><br>Bags<br>Boxes<br>Bottles<br>Cans/Tins<br>Hang Cards<br>Wraps | Color printout<br><br>Color transparency<br><br>Custom C-print<br><br>Cibachrome® print | Transparencies and C-prints of package mockups are persuasive. Photograph multiple packages to better simulate the retail environment. |
| Television Graphics<br><br>Storyboard<br>Identity Slides<br>Infographic<br>Set Design | Marker indication<br><br>Color photocopy<br><br>Color printout<br><br>Color transparency<br><br>Cibachrome® print | Marker indication is best for film, video storyboards. When converting electronic images to hard copy, check for color accuracy. |

# Creative Resume

*Designing Creative Resumes,* a useful companion to this book by Crisp Publications, dissects the resume, examines its function and applications and helps you create a powerful support document. Your resume is viewed as a verbal tool to help get you interviews. It also serves an introduction function during your interview and as a reminder reference after the interview is complete.

You need to develop an exceptional resume to help stage your creative portfolio. It must stimulate an employer to meet and interview you. It should make an unforgettable visual impression. It must establish your credibility, document your past and predict your future. Your creative resume needs to identify you and your work after the interview when you and your portfolio are no longer present.

What direction should your resume take? Certainly package yourself as a unique creative individual. Clarify the benefits an employer will realize when hiring you. Select a comfortable format that will help deliver critical data.

The reverse chronological (latest data first) format places emphasis on your most recent education, employment and activities. This is an excellent approach for young designers with limited experience, as it helps focus on the leading edge of your career development. The reverse chronological format features strategic titles briefly embellished with responsibilities and accomplishments.

An interesting version of this format is the timeline resume which accounts for a specific portion of your career (usually ten years). The timeline, organized as a matrix, is effective for demonstrating consistent progress towards a goal over an extended period. This resume format offers a fertile option for aspiring exhibit, publication or environmental graphic designers, as timeline interpretation is quite common in these specialized areas.

Use the narrative resume format to tell an interesting story about yourself. This style allows you to de-emphasize facts and dates while featuring process and results. Narrative resumes present an opportunity to demonstrate excellent writing. A word ad, script or storyboard for yourself might establish a logical narrative direction. Explore this format if your goal is to work in advertising, publications, film or the electronic media.

The achievement (functional) resume format is generally more useful for experienced rather than young designers. You focus on positive accomplishments including leadership responsibilities, funds managed or goals met. Job titles, work history and repetitive positions are subordinate to verifiable results. Designers find this resume format more useful for redirecting their career or aspiring to a senior position.

To maximize your leverage on a specific design position consider a targeted resume. This format requires your all-out effort because a separate unique resume is created for each position. Targeted resumes depend on solid research and desktop technology. By careful editing you can make a powerful case for a specific job, eliminating data that would be necessary on a more general document.

*achieved*
*analyzed*
*arranged*
*created*
*conducted*
*constructed*
*coordinated*
*delivered*
*designed*
*developed*
*directed*
*established*
*exhibited*
*evaluated*
*gained*
*generated*
*implemented*
*improved*
*increased*
*managed*
*motivated*
*narrated*
*negotiated*
*operated*
*organized*
*planned*
*prepared*
*presented*
*produced*
*promoted*
*realized*
*researched*
*strengthened*
*supervised*
*tested*
*trained*
*upgraded*
*utilized*

What information should your resume contain? An employment objective is an option. If you use one make it concise but suggest flexibility. "Job title" objectives such as Senior Package Designer, Corporate Identification Project Manager or Environmental Graphic Designer suggest both position and level. Avoid paragraph length objectives. These will probably be viewed as too specific. You may risk removing yourself from final consideration for attractive positions.

Document your education or training carefully. Success in college often predicts your future job performance. List all relevant data in reverse chronological order. Include your college degrees with year conferred. Mention creative course clusters and degree minors. Adjust any obscure academic course titles to conform with professional terminology.

Weave in your extraordinary grade point average or class standing. Consider noting, if appropriate, the percentage of your college expenses earned. Remember your relevant extension courses, training seminars and workshops.

Today's employers are interested in your level of computer literacy. Consider a special heading to detail your operating mastery of software programs and hardware systems. List the version of software and computer model to communicate this information clearly. Another way to suggest your computer fluency is to prepare both a print resume and an electronic version. Your electronic resume can be mailed as a disk or CD, and perhaps loaded on Internet to reach a broad international audience.

Professional experience will be carefully examined by potential employers. List your latest position first with all others in reverse order. Show job title, employer, date and responsibilities. For your first creative resume, don't overlook summer positions, part time work and volunteer experiences. Internships and co-op positions should be carefully documented but in a separate category.

Awards, memberships, scholarships, exhibitions and publications are resume categories that showcase the depth and excellence of your educational and professional involvement. The titles "honors" or "activities" may permit you to combine these data entries on a first resume. Later resumes should list complete documentation in each category.

Personal information identifies the creative resume. Your name, address and telephone number need to be easily located in a quick visual scan by any reviewer. Be careful not to disguise this data. Make it obvious for a potential employer to find your phone number and call you. Additional personal information may include age, marital status, health, military status, interests and hobbies. None of these entries is critical. Some may even invade your privacy. When in doubt, omit this peripheral personal data.

References are best not included on your creative resume, but are vital to the process. Be sure to obtain permission to use three references who really know your creative ability, portfolio and work habits. List their names, titles and addresses. Both office and home telephone numbers are important to include. Design a separate reference card or page compatible with your resume. Distribute your reference information only upon special request as the interview process moves toward a sincere job offer.

**nancy** zeches

1553 finch way

sunnyvale, california  94087

408.735.1530

*education*

Bachelor of Arts Degree in Communication Design
Minor in Business Administration
California State University, Chico, 1991

| | |
|---|---|
| Corporate Identity | Advertising |
| Publication Design | Marketing |
| Environmental Graphics | Consumer Behavior |
| Packaging | Management |
| Advertising Design | Economics |
| Typography | Accounting |
| Illustration | Finance |
| Photography | Business Law |
| Reprographics | |
| Marker Rendering | |
| Lettering | |

*travel*

Austria

England

France

Germany

Holland

Hungary

Italy

Portugal

Spain

Switzerland

Yugoslavia

*activities/honors*

First place in ADAC Student Poster Competition, 1991
Graphic Design Scholarship, 1989

Designers In Progress, CSU Chico, 1988 to 1991
(President 1989 and Program Director 1990 to 1991)
Women in Communications, 1988 to 1991
(President 1989)
Impulse Magazine Assistant Art Director, CSU Chico, Fall 1990
(Best of Show)
Workshop with Brian Collentine, CSU Chico, Spring 1991
Workshop with Craig Frazier, CSU Chico, Fall 1989
Envision, ADAC Sacramento, 1989, 1990, 1991
Advertising Club of San Francisco Workshop, 1989, 1990

American Institute of Graphic Arts, 1991 to present
(Serving on the Environmental Committee)
Art Director and Artists Club of Sacramento, 1988 to present

*mac*

Adobe
Illustrator

Adobe
Photoshop

Aldus
Freehand

Aldus
PageMaker

Quark
Express

*employment/internships*

CKS Partners
Freelance, 1991 to present
San Francisco, California

Landor Associates
Graphic Design Intern, 1991 to present
San Francisco, California

Instructional Media Center
Graphic Designer, 1990 to 1991
California State University, Chico, California

Center for Regional and Continuing Education
Graphic Design Intern, 1989 to 1990
California State University, Chico, California

Jerry Kuyper

1595 La Vereda Road
Berkeley, California 94708

510 548 3314

| | | |
|---|---|---|
| 1992 - | Creative Director | frogdesign<br>Menlo Park, California |

**Responsible** for creating corporate/brand identities, packaging, collateral and product identification

**Directed** projects for EO, Elecom, Hexaglot, Jenaglas, Motorola, 3M and Zenith Data Systems

| | | |
|---|---|---|
| 1983 - 1992 | Design Director, Principal | Landor Associates<br>San Francisco, California |

**Managed** projects and directed design for all phases of corporate identity programs including new business presentations, analysis, visual audits, concept development, presentations, design refinement, system development, documentation, introduction and program reviews. Designed and directed development of systems and standards for stationery, forms, checks, credit cards, packaging, signage, vehicles, brochures and advertising. Responsibilities included writing and reviewing proposals, scheduling, meeting profit objectives, making client presentations, reviewing portfolios and recruiting key talent.

**Directed** projects for over forty clients including AT&T, US Sprint, DuPont, GE, Times Mirror, Rizzoli, Fuji Bank, Union Bank, Hawaiian Airlines, Stanford University, World Wildlife Fund, Disney and the 1996 Olympic Games in Atlanta

**Designed** identities for over ten clients including Touchstone Films, Carter Hawley Hale, DuPont, US Sprint, Times Mirror, Avondale Industries and Singapore Technologies

**Selected** approximately twenty interns per year as Chair of the Outreach Committee

**Established** Landor Environmental Committee

**Wrote** article for *Step-By-Step Graphics* on Typography in Corporate Identity

**Presented** the GE Case History at the Design Management Institute Conference on Corporate Identity

| | | |
|---|---|---|
| 1981 - 1983 | Senior Graphic Designer | Saul Bass/Herb Yager & Associates<br>Los Angeles, California |

**Created** design concepts for corporate identities for AT&T, Atari and Warner Communications

**Completed** extensive design development and refinements on the AT&T symbol

| | | |
|---|---|---|
| 1980 - 1981 | Senior Graphic Designer | Office of Richard Saul Wurman<br>Los Angeles, California |

**Developed** informational graphic design for folders, posters, exhibits and guide books

**Designed** numerous maps and established page formats for the first Access Guidebook, *LA Access*

| | | |
|---|---|---|
| 1979 - 1980 | Visiting Professor | National Institute of Design<br>Ahmedabad, India |

**Awarded** a Fulbright-Hays Grant to teach letterform design for one semester

**Visited** twelve countries on a nine month journey around the world

| | | |
|---|---|---|
| 1976 - 1979 | Assistant Professor of Design | University of Hawaii at Manoa<br>Honolulu, Hawaii |

| | | |
|---|---|---|
| 1972 - 1976 | Postgraduate, Graphic Design | Basel School of Design<br>Basel, Switzerland |

| | | |
|---|---|---|
| 1966 - 1971 | Graduate, Graphic Design | University of Cincinnati<br>Cincinnati, Ohio |

# Cover
# Letter

If you mail your resume, be sure to include a cover letter for explanation and support. If you fax it be sure to also fax a cover. Your cover letter helps personalize your message to an employer. Mail only to a specific individual in the organization. Include his or her job title. Never mail to the firm name only; to do so will further dilute your resume's power. Think of the cover letter as your personal introduction. Treat it as if you were describing yourself briefly on the telephone. Communicate your potential value to the firm. Stimulate the employer's curiosity. Provoke a need to know more about you and to generate a response.

Each time you mail or fax a resume, write a unique cover letter. Perfect grammar and spelling are expected. Typing or laser printing should be flawless. Develop a solid content structure, but personalize each letter. Avoid formula cover letters in which only the address changes. Employers will easily spot the transparency of your effort. Beware of photocopied cover letters as they are seen as duplicates, not originals.

Produce your cover letters on paper that complements your creative resume. If the resume stock will not accept photocopying or laser printing, at least match color and finish. Another approach is to select a coordinated letterhead and envelope that tastefully contrasts with your resume. White paper is always appropriate.

Adopt a proven block style business letter format. Have someone carefully proof your cover letters. Pay particular attention to spelling the name of your interview target. Sign your name neatly in a color other than black. Direct mail experts have found that a dark blue signature stimulates superior reader response. Be sure to add the enclosure indication to enhance the professional appearance of your creative cover letters.

Keep your cover letter short. Never exceed a single page unless you seek a writing position. Three or four precise, economical paragraphs are adequate.

The opening paragraph is critical. Attract attention with something interesting about the firm or, better yet, the reader. Be timely. Show that you are informed about the company. Mention some recent work of prominence. Comment on a current article by or about the employer. Praise a professional award. Make connections between a reference, the employer and you. Mention why you are writing. Indicate here if you are responding to an advertisement or placement tip.

Paragraph two might contain a teaser about your resume to stimulate the employer to read it thoroughly. Mention your college, degree, year and study focus if you are a recent graduate. Touch on your significant experience. Three or four sentences will suffice.

Use paragraph three to create a special interest in you. Connect your unique skills to the needs of an employer. Even if no position exists, this paragraph must tantalize the employer to want to meet you. No easy task, these few sentences require a strong research base. Project yourself as unique and valuable.

The last paragraph should close the sale. Use it to suggest an interview. Ask for a review of your portfolio. Be sure to mention that you will be calling to arrange a personal meeting. By promising to telephone, you have already broken ground for future messages. This action oriented closing statement allows you to retain the initiative and exploit the momentum of the job search process.

**Bart Corzine** D e s i g n          23 Bidwell Circle          Telephone
                                        Chico, California 95926          916.898.6688

May 23, 1995

Mr. Craig Renwick
Design Director
Graphus, Inc.
1527 Trimble Tower
Chicago, IL 60601

Dear Mr. Renwick:

It was a pleasure to meet with you briefly at the ACD Conference in Chicago last October. In our conversation you suggested that I send you a resume upon graduation. Your presentation, "Kinetic Typography" was for me the highlight of the Saturday session. You brought clarity and focus to an important topic seldom discussed. The conference provided my first opportunity to experience Chicago. I was really moved by the extraordinary architecture, the fine museums and the city's lakefront beauty. After learning more of the dynamic graphic design community and strong professional organizations, Chicago became my top career destination.

While at CSU/Chico I studied under two of your former colleagues, Professor Berryman and Professor Cahill who encouraged me to contact your firm. The CSU/Chico design program features strong emphasis on typography, information design and methodology, integrated with interactive technology. Two internships with Wise Design in Santa Rosa and Landor Associates in San Francisco required collaborative design and helped to refine my computer skills.

The high quality work of Graphus is familiar through recent articles in *Novum*, *Eye* and *Communication Arts.* An exhibit of your corporate identity projects at our university in February helped me establish empathy with the Graphus design direction. My professional goal has long been to work in a major market with a top creative team like Graphus.

I will be in Chicago during the first week in June to attend the AIGA "Design Into the Future" symposium. Early Monday morning, June 4th, I will telephone to schedule a portfolio review during the week.

I look forward to meeting with you at your convenience.

Sincerely,

*Bart Corzine*

Bart Corzine

ENC: Resume

# Portfolio Reminders

Graphic reminders can provide a valuable supplement to your package of creative portfolio, resume and cover letter. Illustrators and photographers have historically mailed innovative promotional pieces to creative directors. Frequent mailings help keep their names and work before important buyers and decision makers. You might build on this tradition to follow up your creative interviews.

Self-promos help you maintain contact with your interview targets. Perhaps you had encouraging feedback but a position was not open during your initial interview. Mail a reminder. Maybe you were called back for a second or third meeting but the project that would determine your hiring was delayed. Send a reminder. You are in a holding pattern in a lesser position but want to move up to that dream slot when it opens. Maintain contact with a mailer. Circumstances force you to change your address and telephone. Spread the news with an innovative self-promotional mailer.

Why do graphic reminders work? Creative directors live in a world of fresh ideas. Many are avid collectors of graphic ephemera. They enjoy being entertained. However, your reminder must communicate quickly. The decision to trash it, hang it or file it will be reached in just a few seconds. Your mailer must be provocative or it will vanish.

Remember, the primary function of your graphic reminder is to help a creative director recall you and your portfolio. It should enhance your identity, trigger positive impressions and extend the interview event. Your self-promotion might also add conceptual dimension to your book.

Portfolio reminders need not be expensive to reproduce. You might include them on the same press sheet as your resume/reference/thank you system. Sharp laserprints or photocopies will also work. Postcards or greeting cards can be effective. Seasonal or holiday cards are appropriate if your timing is right. Signed original art and photo reminders are difficult for anyone to discard.

Consider mailing three or four 35 mm slides of your strongest portfolio pieces with a business card. Enclose slides, tearsheets or samples of work created *after* your interview. Perhaps package only your business card in a unique envelope, box or bottle. An appropriate self-portrait might spark memories of your work. Reminders can take many forms but must be designed to make it easy for the creative director to contact you.

If portfolio reminders seem right for you, consider designing a set or series. This opens the possibility of multiple mailings. Try mailing to the creative director on four consecutive days, each piece a variation on your graphic theme. Perhaps a weekly mailing will demonstrate your persistence and continued interest in a position. When you are confident that your portfolio reminders have arrived, follow up with a telephone call to update your status.

**Consider a practical size for your direct mail promotion. Pieces larger than 8 1/2×11" not only substantially increase your shipping costs, but are also less likely to be retained, filed and referred to by the art director. Your mailing envelope is as important as its contents. Make it enticing and tie it in thematically with your promo. For a calligraphy promotion, I hand lettered one thousand envelopes. Art directors saved them as well as the promo inside.**

Brenda Walton
Principal
Brenda Walton
Calligraphy and Illustration
Sacramento, CA

# LES
# IS
# MOORE

REACH **LES MOORE** AT 312.585-5283

# LESS
# IS
# MOORE

REACH **LES MOORE** AT 312.585-5283

# MOORE
# OR
# LESS

REACH **LES MOORE** AT 312.585-5283

# MOORE
# IS
# MORE

REACH **LES MOORE** AT 312.585-5283

# Portfolio Etiquette

The creative portfolio is a strategic tool. To work for you it must be packaged with a sound plan to market yourself. A magnificent portfolio is useless if it rests quietly in storage under your bed or on a shelf in the garage. Your portfolio needs to be shown to help you land that coveted project or position. Techniques to maximize the unique impact of your creative work involve portfolio etiquette.

Building your portfolio is a formidable task. Completing it will bring pride and satisfaction. However, only the act of presenting it will help achieve your real objective, a challenging position or project. Consider your creative portfolio to be the key ingredient of your job search. Combined with a powerful resume and a solid marketing plan, your portfolio will document your capabilities and predict future job performance.

Focus your attention on scheduling interviews by telephone or letter. Be prepared to use both techniques to match the accepted scheduling process in your target market.

Corporations, rich in tradition, may have more formal interviewing policies than fast-growing start-up companies. International advertising agencies observe more traditional protocol than regional consulting firms. West Coast etiquette differs from that observed in Boston, Atlanta, New York City or London. Telephone the AIGA or Art Directors group in your target market to inquire about local interviewing expectations, dress codes and portfolio drop-off customs.

Time of year is critical when scheduling interviews. July and August are often difficult, since these are the favorite vacation months of decision makers. June probably has the greatest influx of university graduates entering the job market. The Christmas holidays are uncertain, due to vacations and travel. Annual report season and tax season can be so hectic internally that many firms find little time for interviewing. Publishing firms are in chaos during the days preceding print deadlines.

Time your interview campaign to coincide with peak hiring periods. The September, October and November months are best for finding creative positions, followed closely by the first quarter of the year.

The most direct interview method is to arrange an appointment by telephone. You might get lucky and talk directly to the person who will ultimately interview you. A brief friendly conversation can help warm things up for your interview.

Probably your call will reach a receptionist or creative secretary. It is critical to recognize the important role that secretaries, studio managers and receptionists fill in the interview process. Make friends with them! Treat them with the utmost courtesy and respect. They are the gatekeepers to the creative directors who ultimately interview you. Obnoxious telephone demeanor or condescending office behavior will virtually guarantee that you will not receive an interview.

Voice mail is a technology used by some creative firms to collect incoming telephone calls for answering at a convenient time. Prepare, in writing, a powerful voice mail response. Craft it carefully. Keep it friendly and informative—but brief. Pace and volume are critical. Be sure to repeat your telephone number—slowly—along with a contact time.

Get as much information about potential employers and clients as possible. The office receptionist and/or secretary can provide a great wealth of knowledge. With one simple phone call you can get insight into office protocol, studio attire and even the personalities of the principals.
Dino Paul
Design Director
After Hours Agency
Phoenix, AZ

**When calling for interviews you never know who you may be talking with and how much influence they may have on your future. Leave a good impression. Be polite. Show respect. Your attitude will be a major factor in "getting your portfolio in the door."**
Ann Burris
Studio Manager
The Dunlavey Studio
Sacramento, CA

*The Cake* (What I expect). **That your book is neat, clean and ordered. That your work reflects talent, passion and education.**
*The Frosting* (What I search for). **Have patience. Understand that designers are very busy and may not see your work on the first or even second go round . . . it's not you! If you are gracious and understanding about your appointment being pushed back or rescheduled, you'll gain my respect.**
Lisa Smedley
Studio Manager
Gensler Associates
San Francisco

To beat the executive telephone guards try calling before 8 a.m., during lunch, after 5 p.m. or on Saturday morning. Decision-makers often come by the office early, work through lunch, after hours and even on weekends. Try to reach these busy executives when they are apt to be answering their own phones. Calls made during off hours are less likely to interrupt important office business.

If your phone call hits target, keep your conversation short and direct. Be positive, courteous and complimentary. Encourage the interviewer to set a specific interview time. If the firm is extremely busy, suggest a time at the end of the normal working day. Then the work pace slows, telephones stop ringing, and you will receive more time and attention. Try to avoid Mondays, the most hectic day of the week for many interviewers.

You may be asked to mail in your resume before an interview will be confirmed. Employers scan the resume to screen your credibility and qualifications, saving precious interview time for the really serious job seekers. Design your creative resume to pass this tough review and set the stage for a face-to-face meeting.

A second method for scheduling an interview is to mail a resume accompanied by a cover letter. This technique affords you sufficient time to compose a strategic letter, tailored to each employer. Addressed to a creative director in the firm, the letter will usually reach that person without interference. Never address this package to only the company name. Never mail your resume without a cover letter. Aim your creative resume directly at your job target to improve your chances for an interview.

Another way to set up an interview is to coordinate mailing with a telephone call. For this technique to work well you need to accurately predict delivery. If the postal schedule is uncertain, use a registered letter or courier service to guarantee delivery and attract the attention of an employer. Simply mail your resume with cover letter and call the day of delivery or the day after to request an interview. An impression of your resume should be fresh in the mind of an employer during the telephone conversation. This technique allows you to demonstrate organization and planning skills. At the same time you can show an employer the importance you attach to the meeting.

Whether arranging interviews by telephone or mail, avoid asking directly if any jobs are available, positions are open or hiring is taking place. Creative positions tend to be filled in unusual style. Rather than ask for a job, ask for a review of your portfolio. Most creative supervisors and art directors find empathy with your eagerness, having previously experienced it themselves. They enjoy interviewing during slack work periods; in fact, part of their job is to discover new talent. If you take this approach, the least you will get is valuable feedback. In addition you are apt to receive employment leads and reference approval. Don't worry about a job offer. It will come naturally if you and your creative portfolio make a positive and lasting impression.

# Design
# Networking

Michael Kennedy, a prominent Sacramento creative director with a long and continued interest in advising young designers, is a strong advocate of networking. "If you are looking for a job in the graphic design field, don't sit around and wait for the telephone to ring. Being in the right place at the right time is critical in landing a good position. This means meeting as many people as you can."

Start by building contacts early in your student years. Be sure to meet and stay in touch with outstanding senior students. They make wonderful resources as you progress in your design program and valuable professional contacts when you graduate. Most design schools have student organizations which afford opportunities to interact outside the classroom. Assume a leadership position if you are so inclined. Perhaps help arrange for speakers' visits. Take the time to talk with visiting alumni, guest lecturers and show judges. Other valuable contacts can be made while on class field trips to studios, agencies, printers and vendors.

Effective networking begins when you join the creative professional organization in your target market. If your focus is graphic design, the American Institute of Graphic Arts (AIGA, New York) has chapters in most major cities. The American Center for Design (ACD, Chicago) maintains both a regional and national membership. Local Art Directors' Clubs in major media markets have active rosters and full calendars of events. While membership fees may seem a bit high to young designers, club benefits are numerous. Most useful are the job listings and placement services available only to members. Club directories reveal who's who in your market. Mailings, guest speakers and award shows all provide opportunities to make valuable contacts.

Networking consistently confirms the adage "It's not what you know but who you know." A good contact will not guarantee a position but will get you an interview where you can sell yourself. Do not overlook friends of your family as you begin your job search. Your family banker, attorney, realtor, stockbroker or physician may be a source of contacts. Check with family relatives and friends in your target market. They may be familiar with local designers, printers, developers, editors or corporate executives who will help with your search.

Alumni networking can be fruitful for young designers. Strong design programs keep careful track of their alumni and rely on them to help recent graduates with references, interviews and internships. Your design professors will help guide you to alumni practicing in your target market. Graduate directories, university magazines and department newsletters are other reliable sources of alumni data.

Another method of developing contacts is to join local service organizations, community arts groups, charitable societies or political campaigns. Serving on city commissions, museum boards, gallery support groups and special event committees will help develop contacts over time. Don't hesitate to volunteer, it is a rewarding way to enlarge your circle of contacts while serving your community.

Conferences, social gatherings and design club meetings are some of the events at which you can make the personal contacts that are necessary in this business. Don't be shy. Introduce yourself and keep in touch with people. Follow up. You never know who that one person might be who in turn recommends you for the perfect design job.
Michael Kennedy
Designer/Instructor
Michael Kennedy Associates
Sacramento, CA

# Placement Professionals

**We are always looking for stars, since those are the types of designers and design managers we are paid to find by our clients. So, show us what you do better (or have directed) than anyone else—in an extremely neat, well-thought out, and organized manner.**
RitaSue Siegel
Chairman
RitaSue Siegel Associates
Recruiting Consultants
New York City

---

**Display a broad spectrum of the work you've done. Ten pieces of your best work may not be as reflective of all your skills as ten diverse selections. Flexibility and adaptability can be as important as talent in this volatile industry.**
Diane Pirritino
Managing Director
T-Square, etc.
Design Placement
Los Angeles

One alternative to selling yourself in the job market is to secure the services of a placement firm specializing in graphic design. These professional headhunters are located in New York, Boston, Chicago and Los Angeles but market their services nationally and internationally. Specific addresses are listed in the reference section of this book. Placement consultants maintain close contact with prominent design offices and advertising agencies. When an open position is filled, a fee is paid by the employer directly to the placement firm at no charge to the designer.

Placement professionals perform a valuable function for both employer and employee. Employers benefit from the matchmaking and screening skills of the agency. Designers benefit from a focused job search, prearranged interviews and experienced salary negotiation. Placement firms interview designers to evaluate their resumes and portfolios. They are particularly adept at assessing career goals and helping target specific firms and markets.

Working with a placement professional does not relieve the designer of the responsibility of producing an exceptional portfolio. Exhibiting shoddy work on your placement interview will certainly disqualify you from the process. The reputation of the placement firm is at stake. With high standards, they can afford to recommend only qualified and innovative designers for top positions. While most agencies will take on exceptional graduates right out of design school, experienced professionals tend to be in greater demand.

# Interview
# Research

After you identify your ideal market, develop a careful research plan to select the studios, agencies or corporations worth interviewing. Plan for about 20 interviews. It will take at least that number to expose you and your work to the market. Exhaust your list before taking on another group of firms. Management, scheduling and communication problems compound when your interview list grows too lengthy.

Start by joining the local creative professional organization (American Institute of Graphic Arts, American Center for Design, Art Directors Club) to benefit from placement services available only to members. The membership lists and regular professional events will accelerate your understanding of the market. Telephone yellow pages provide an accurate, timely cross-reference of firms to interview.

Record your interview target firms on large index cards or on Job Search Record Forms photocopied from the following page. List telephone numbers, addresses, names of the creative directors and receptionists. Large agencies and consulting firms often assign a creative secretary to schedule interviews. As your interviews progress, note pertinent names, dates, times and comments. Update your files and treat these forms as the primary reference for your search. Keeping your interview information organized is well worth your time investment.

Prioritize your list by arranging references in your order of preference. Plan to interview only after you collect significant data on each studio, agency or corporation.

Research the size of the organization, the number of offices and important clients. Learn the age of your target company and the names of the CEO and principals. Study the annual report if available. If publicly held, check the value of the corporate common stock. Ask about the reputation of the firm and how its employees are treated.

Research plays a major role in your self-directed job search. Creative positions are seldom listed in newspaper classified sections. Most openings are filled through word of mouth and by personal referral in the creative underground. A handful of highly specialized placement agencies and headhunters focus on experienced personnel. Timing and luck also play a major role. Account changes, new clients, contract awards and business cycle changes all contribute to job availability.

Careful research of target firms and their representatives will prepare you to interview intelligently. You will not have to ask redundant questions during the interview. You will demonstrate that you are truly prepared and have more than just a casual interest in the organization. More important, being informed will boost your confidence and help you make a strong impression.

Be very patient once you begin interviewing. Word travels fast on the creative grapevine, when you make it known that you're available. Even if you receive a job offer after your first or second interview, follow your game plan. Other offers may be more attractive. By interviewing all of your targets, you start to build your reputation in the market. Value the contacts you make during your search. These individuals may be future colleagues or employers if you change positions.

**Know your audience and prepare your portfolio accordingly. Although it requires more effort, a presentation which targets the specific needs or interests of the viewer almost always fares better than its generic counterpart.**
Doug Powell
President
Powell and Associates
Atlanta

**If you are really serious about wanting to work for my firm, one way you can impress me is to spend some extra time before your interview to design a comp for one of my major clients. Keep it simple . . . one or two colors or maybe a black and white ad to show how you think. Another suggestion is to make a copy of something already in your portfolio and alter it by applying my client's name and logo.**
Michael Kennedy
Designer/Instructor
Michael Kennedy Associates
Sacramento, CA

# Job Search
# Record Form

## STUDIO/AGENCY/CORPORATION

NAME

ADDRESS

CITY/STATE/ZIP

TELEPHONE

FAX

DESIGN DIRECTOR

RECEPTIONIST

OWNER

## TARGET POSITION

## ACTION      DATE

◯   MAILED RESUME

◯   CALL BACK

◯   INTERVIEW

◯   MAILED SELF-PROMO

## FEEDBACK

PORTFOLIO

RESUME

## JOB LEADS FROM INTERVIEW

## RESEARCH SOURCES

PERSONAL REFERENCES

BOOKS/PERIODICALS

EXHIBITIONS

ANNUAL REPORT

## EXPENSES

# Creative
# Interview

Your creative interview is the big event. Dress for it. Select your clothing for a job level higher than the one you seek. Although interviewers in creative professions may dress less formally than their corporate or banking counterparts, you should aim for a stylish, conservative appearance. Your suit or outfit should be reserved and businesslike. Dark colors make the best initial impression. Select your necktie or accessories carefully. Appear clean, neat and well-groomed. Keep jewelry, perfume and aftershave scents subtle. Never smoke or chew gum. Look professional and ready to begin work at the time of your creative interview.

On the day of your interview arise early from a good night's sleep. Read the daily newspaper thoroughly. Scan *USA Today* or the *Wall Street Journal* for topical events. Or perhaps watch the morning television news. This last bit of preparation might help to lead into the interview and demonstrate that you are particularly informed, aware and interested.

Be on time for your interview; better yet, arrive 15 minutes early. Plan two or three hours between appointments for recovery time and transportation contingencies. Your interview may last longer than planned, particularly if the employer is really interested. While waiting, you might chat with the receptionist or secretary. Be careful not to interrupt any conversations or tasks that might be under way. Positive impressions you make at the front desk will build a solid foundation for your successful interview.

As you begin to interview, present your resume, even though you may have sent one through the mail. Expect the employer to glance down at your document and take notes throughout the interview process. Let the interviewer lead and pace the conversation. Be prepared to expand on your resume data. Your creative resume helps guide the opening phase of your interview.

As you face your host, radiate an enthusiastic self-confidence. Smile and maintain eye contact. While seated, express your alertness with positive body language. Try to appear relaxed and comfortable while maintaining an assured posture.

When the conversation turns to your portfolio, prepare to answer questions about your work. Briefly describe the problem and your rationale for each solution you present. Plan to defend your visual decisions. Talk articulately about typography, marketing constraints and production possibilities. Never make excuses for your work, a sure sign of weakness. Your creative portfolio must succeed at face value and speak for itself.

Handling your creative portfolio is an issue. One interviewer might want to take total control and hold each piece. Another may prefer that you take each plate out of your case and replace it. A third might be interested in thumbing through only sketchbooks or publications. You need to read the inclination of each reviewer and make them feel comfortable during the interview. Remember, these are people who have handled hundreds or even thousands of portfolios. Trust them to treat your portfolio with clean hands and respect.

The ideal pacing of your portfolio will add value to your work. If you present your concepts too quickly, your solutions will seem less important. Prolonging the sequence will bore your reviewer. Think of each solution as the precious item it is, the culmination of your investment of time and money. Each plate or page is a valuable asset. Your task is to market this package of assets confidently at each interview.

**Dress for a business presentation . . . not for the campus. Be persuasive. Make sure there are no misspelled words in your written materials.**
John. P. Carlson
Principal
Carlson Associates
Sacramento, CA

**Be prepared to discuss the intent of every piece in your portfolio. Don't assume your portfolio will speak for itself. It is your career after all, and you should anticipate explaining and defending the thought that went into your portfolio.**
Al Zimmerman
Owner/Designer
The Zimmerman Group
Bellingham, WA

**While most portfolios contain primarily finished printed work, I highly recommend including some presentation mock-ups. Talk about each mock-up as though presenting a new idea to a client. You may have the highest level of creativity, but if you cannot articulate and present (sell) your ideas at the mock-up phase, you will not succeed.**
Pat Davis
Principal
Pat Davis Design
Sacramento, CA

**When showing your portfolio, demonstrate your abilities to problem seek. Orally present each design solution by describing the assignment as given by your professor, client or ad executive. Then describe the redefining and focusing which resulted from your research.**

Wendy T. Olmstead
Assistant Professor
Visual Communication
Purdue University
Lafayette, IN

**Be proud of your work and accomplishments. Never tell a prospective employer that you would do something "differently" from the work you are showing. If you have a piece in question, take it out of your portfolio or revise it so that you are proud to show it.**

Jill Howry
President
Russell, Howry & Associates
San Francisco

**Always leave an interview with three names of other people to see or companies to talk with. Word of mouth is one of your best sources for gaining contacts.**

Michelle Shibata-Schwartz
Principal
Shibata-Schwartz Design
San Francisco

Do not interrupt your interviewer, a most annoying habit. Yet feel free to ask questions. This is a valuable opportunity to reflect your preliminary research. Ask about key personnel. Request information on significant work in process. Inquire about corporate growth. Most experienced interviewers are flattered by good questions if you phrase them properly. Praise high profile projects produced by the firm if you truly respect the results.

A good way to anticipate and prepare for interviewing is to role-play with a critical friend, your professor or college placement personnel. Rehearse for the creative interview to ease your anxieties. Many colleges offer video facilities that enable you to view practice interviews and improve your performance. Your professors probably have professional contacts who will help you with a dress rehearsal. Take advantage of practice opportunities to help you through the first two or three appointments. After those initial experiences you will feel more comfortable.

Self-assessment questions are likely to arise during your interview. What can you do for us? What results have you produced? Why would you want to work here? Why should we hire you? Where would you like to be in five years? These frequently asked cliches can be very revealing. Prepare a few short, creative responses. Rehearse them and you'll pass with flying colors.

At an opportune time in the interview emphasize precisely how you might help the company. Stress your unique qualifications. Draw a connection between yourself and the firm. Explain how you might fit the organization and add to it. Avoid asking directly for a job, but try to sell yourself so convincingly that the interviewer will feel obligated to discuss hiring.

When you sense the interview is about to end, request some feedback. You may not even have to ask, since criticism is part of the standard language of creative professionals. Some interviewers will be kind and constructive. Others will be polite but aloof. A few might be harsh and cynical. Accept any comments gracefully. Avoid arguments even if you vehemently disagree. Remember that criticism is only the opinion of one person. You will receive a balanced picture of the strengths and weaknesses of your portfolio by comparing the comments of several reviewers. Feedback, when taken as advice, can only improve your next opportunity. Use each critique to help modify your portfolio, refine your target research and streamline your responses.

Close the interview on a positive note. A warm thank you, confident eye contact and a firm handshake are in order before leaving. Successful closure involves more than just a cordial parting. Find out where you stand. Suggest that you will keep in touch by telephone. Ask the interviewer to recommend a colleague or another firm that might benefit from your work. Many fine positions are located from these special leads. Indicate your availability for a future interview. Leave a positive lasting impression with your interest, sincerity and persuasiveness. Follow the interview with a brief thank-you note or letter to complete the creative interview.

# Negotiating Strategies

If you make a positive impression, your timing is fortunate, and a position is open, an offer may come your way. A typical employment offer will indicate your job title, starting salary, probation period, training program, working hours, employee benefits and required travel.

You will need to decide if the offer measures up to your expectations. Will it allow you to survive in your target market as you begin your career? A good test is to build an honest monthly budget. List your projected housing, food, utilities, transportation, insurance and clothing expenses. Chart your medical coverage, taxes and savings. Do not forget to include your educational loan repayment. Also plan for state and federal withholding.

This budget plan will help compare your job offer with reality. You can hardly expect to buy a Mercedes, build your dream home and retire in comfort after a year on the job. However, if food stamps are necessary for you to exist between paychecks, the offer is too low.

Prepare yourself to negotiate salary. Telephone local professional design societies to determine the beginning salary range in your market. The *Graphic Artists Guild Pricing and Ethical Guidelines* publishes annual comparative compensation rates for the United States . . . *How*, *Print* and *Communication Arts* magazines conduct periodic salary surveys. Each market will vary. No single magic starting salary exists. But you need to grasp the salary range in your job category before you interview. It is wise to calculate your value in dollars per hour. Ten dollars per hour based on a 40 hour work week yields less than $20,000 gross per year. Beginning designers are often better off working on an hourly basis than on salary, as long hours are common in your first position.

If you are asked to name your salary requirements, politely decline. Wait until your interviewer makes an offer. As a rule employers offer higher salary figures than employees themselves quote. You can be sure that an open position has already been budgeted. Maneuver the employer to quote the salary range for the position (which you already know from your research). Then begin your negotiation at the top of the scale to improve your strategic bargaining posture.

If the interviewer absolutely insists that you name your starting salary, quote a figure comfortably above the range. You can always bargain down to the top of the range. If the tone is "We start all junior designers at $25,000 a year," then this presents an opportunity for you to review your special qualifications. Do not hesitate to ask if the fixed number is negotiable. The probe might pay off.

Your ability to negotiate job offers successfully depends on your total self-marketing package. Project the friendly self-confidence of a professional poker player. Sell your portfolio like it contains rare art objects. Position your capabilities above those of other applicants. Clarify the strong conviction you have in your special ability.

Some positions include benefits and perks. Use of an automobile, travel allowance, paid parking, insurance, stock options or profit sharing might sweeten your offer. Healthy benefit packages can help compensate for low starting salaries. Be careful not to make too much fuss about benefits in your initial interview. Let the employer provide the details. Place your primary emphasis on *getting* the position, not haggling over minute details. If you appear too greedy or aggressive the interviewer might be turned off.

Avoid giving your salary expectation during an interview. Let the employer give you the salary range for the position first. Be prepared to give reasons why you should be hired at the top of the range.
Diane M. DiCarlo
President
Negotiation Mastery
Venice, FL

| YEARS | JOB TITLE | ANNUAL RANGE IN $ |
|---|---|---|
| 20 | | |
| 15 | OWNER | 50K/250K |
| 10 | PARTNER | 50K/150K |
| 9 | ASSOCIATE | 50K/100K |
| 8 | CREATIVE DIRECTOR | 50K/100K |
| 7 | | |
| 6 | PROJECT MANAGER | 40K/100K |
| 5 | SENIOR DESIGNER | 25K/50K |
| 4 | | |
| 3 | JUNIOR DESIGNER | 15K/25K |
| 2 | | |
| 1 | DESIGN ASSISTANT | 15K/20K |

**This chart suggests typical job titles, years of work experience and salary ranges for graphic designers employed by top studios, agencies and corporations in major markets. Salary ranges use a 1995 baseline and should be adjusted for inflation. Examine the scale to set your career objectives.**

Beware of accepting any job offer at the time of your initial interview. Postpone your acceptance for a couple of days to analyze the offer. This is a good time to contact your references for their advice. Take this interval to compare other offers. A reasonable gestation period may influence the employer to raise the initial offer, particularly if progress on an important project depends on your hire. The employer may have a fear of losing you. Up to a week is fair to consider an offer. Wait too long and you will lose valuable negotiating leverage.

Starting salary is only one component of employment. More important is your opportunity to work with top creative talent in a stimulating environment. Consider the challenge of the position. Examine your chance for personal growth. Weigh your job responsibilities. Remember that most creative people make frequent job changes early in their careers. Moves are made to gain additional exposure, responsibility and compensation. Initially seek a challenge and rise to it. Financial reward will follow.

If you are fortunate enough to find a position where your daily activities do not seem like work, then your job search will have paid rich dividends. Individuals able to give to a position more than they take from it are lucky indeed. The variety, stimulation and satisfaction of creative design work contributes immensely to your life and to the lives of your family, your co-workers, your community and improving society.

# Portfolio
# Drop-Off

Optimum interview situations place you eyeball to eyeball with employers. Your work is the main topic of conversation. You not only get verbal feedback but are able to read the gestures, expressions and body language of your reviewer. At the conclusion of the interview, criticism is fresh in your mind. You own a golden opportunity to ask professional questions about your performance and pursue additional interview prospects.

The situation is vastly different if your target studio has a "drop-off only" policy. High-profile design offices are often overwhelmed with requests for portfolio reviews. If every interview request were granted, the productivity of the creative team might be reduced or even damaged.

Portfolio drop-off policies are adopted to screen for a few elite candidates who may be scheduled for future interviews. Think of portfolio drop-off as a lottery. Your odds are slim, but if your book sparks attention, the end payoff might make this mysterious process worthwhile.

As a beginning designer, you need to decide if you even want to play the drop-off game. The problem is feedback. Will you really benefit from an interview process that lacks personal contact and direct critical comments about your work? How can you be sure that your problem solutions will be understood without your personal presentation? Will all of your pieces be considered? Will your portfolio case even be opened? These uncertainties of the drop-off process deserve your consideration.

If you decide to try even one portfolio drop-off, some hints may be useful. Remember, once your creative portfolio leaves your hands, you lose control. Your book must clearly communicate your identity, personality and creativity without your presence to support it.

Rather than drop off your portfolio case, you might leave a 35mm, 2 1/4"×2 1/4" or 4×5 transparency portfolio. Forget slide trays, since most busy creative directors find the set-up to be awkward and time consuming. Arrange your slides or transparencies in soft archival page files. Better yet, try the Savage Pre-Vu®, or TransView® mount holders used by professional photographers. These black, rigid, die-cut mounts mask the edges of your transparencies and provide a neutral viewing ground. Identify your visual solutions with concise typeset tags or use a cross reference page. Be sure to attach your business card to the back of each page or board.

If you drop off your portfolio case, identification is critical. Display your name, telephone number and address prominently inside the case. Attach this label to the surface facing your work. A laminated business card securely mounted is sufficient.

Be sure to keep several copies of your resume accessible inside the portfolio. Place them in a pocket facing your work. Perhaps build a pocket board to create an exciting lead-in to your portfolio. Why several resumes? Assume that more than one person will look at your work. Each might want a sample resume. Perhaps a copy or two will be mailed, faxed or passed on to professional colleagues in another agency, studio or corporation.

**There is nothing more critical than your portfolio. Each piece should be stunning and as close to perfection as possible. Your portfolio represents you when you're not there. It is your voice and speaks much louder than your words.**
McRay Magleby
Art Director
Brigham Young University
Provo, UT

When your portfolio speaks for you, it should not apologize. Pay attention to detail, craft and cleanliness. Emphasize quality over quantity and be objective when deciding what to include. Your first impression may be your only one—make it count.
Alan Rellaford
Design Director
Sargent + Berman
Los Angeles

Clearly mark the exterior of your portfolio case. Securely attach a luggage tag sized to your laminated business card. An alternative is to identify your case with one-half-inch adhesive vinyl letters. Attach these to mark the top opening direction. Consider adding a date tag to your case. Offices with drop-off policies will probably have many other portfolios in-house at the same time. Obvious date identification might help keep your book close at hand rather than have it filed away in an obscure office or storage area.

Individual pieces in the portfolio might be identified neatly on the reverse side with a business card. Consider numbering the back of each board to document your preferred sequence. Colorful sticky-back price dots work well. A short descriptive paragraph on each plate can help place your solutions in context. Some reviewers prefer a separate description list for each portfolio piece. Others find cross-referencing sheets awkward. If you decide to include problem descriptions, write with economy, perfect spelling and punctuation. Provide user-friendly type at a minimum size of eight points.

A telephone call will set up a portfolio drop-off. Your work will normally be reviewed during the day or after typical work hours. Some studios prefer to keep your work for a couple of days to fit the review into busy schedules. Some designers set aside a specific day each week or every other week to look at portfolios. Be sure you clearly understand the drop-off policy of each employer. Record the name of the person accepting your book. Pick it up promptly. Check the contents of your portfolio carefully to prepare for your next interview.

What might you expect from a portfolio drop-off? Seldom will you receive a detailed written review of your work. Sometimes a brief paragraph-length check sheet will be included. Perhaps you will receive a thank you form. Often you will receive nothing at all. Do not hesitate to telephone the creative person who evaluated your drop-off book within two or three days. Ask for some frank feedback. The best outcome is an invitation to return and present your portfolio in person.

Be sure to follow up each drop-off with a tasteful thank you note or card. This common courtesy will help reinforce your identity and resume. When in doubt, ask the studio receptionist to whom you might address your written thanks.

The portfolio drop-off procedure might seem awkward and even a waste of time. It can take your portfolio out of your hands (and out of circulation) when you may need it for another interview. Yet it may be the only line of communication open to creative directors in top studios. If you are showing an illustration or photography portfolio, drop-off gives you an opportunity to book some freelance work. However, your chance of landing that dream creative position by this route without follow-up interviews is very remote.

# Graduate School Portfolio

A topnotch portfolio is prerequisite for acceptance into a graduate design program. Other requirements include an exceptional grade point average, a successful Graduate Record Examination score and a detailed resume. Writing skills are verified by an application essay, essential in determining a match between the candidate's goals and the orientation of a particular graduate program. A personal interview is usually required. Most reputable programs insist that candidates complete significant work experience between undergraduate and graduate studies. Some schools accept a percentage of graduates from other disciplines (Fine Art, Psychology, etc.) on the condition that they complete additional study before entering graduate design courses. The Master of Fine Arts degree, Master of Design degree or the Master of Graphic Design degree typically involves two years of resident study (48 to 60 total credit hours) and includes a written thesis documenting original research.

The focus of each graduate program varies according to department philosophy and the faculty in residence. Stronger programs have a core faculty dedicated to graduate design education and a consistent minimum enrollment of at least five students in each graduating group. Curricula requires rigorous study of design history, research methodologies, communication design theory and critical analysis. Graduate studies investigate the underpinnings of graphic design and help students connect academic theory with the evolution of professional practice in graphic design.

Advanced study in graphic design can lead in several exciting directions. Those re-entering professional practice have an enhanced opportunity to work at higher levels for consulting firms of international repute. Graduate study serves as a springboard for some to work on collaborative teams in the research and development sector, with think-tanks, foundations and government agencies. Others are stimulated to publish the results of their graduate investigations, develop software or enter design journalism. Universities, colleges and art schools demand the prerequisite graduate degree to begin a career in design academia.

Applicants to graduate programs should submit a slide portfolio or electronic portfolio for preliminary screening. At the graduate interview you should be prepared to present your portfolio samples in person. The graduate school portfolio should reflect recent work experience, demonstrate refined ideation capabilities, integrate writing into design solutions and show computer literacy. By including exceptional printed samples and process sketches, an accurate assessment can be made of your potential to excel in graduate studies.

Meredith Davis, coordinator of graduate studies in Graphic Design at North Carolina State University and a national authority on graduate design education indicates that content and context are critical in the graduate application portfolio. She adds, "Graduate schools are interested in your possible focus for graduate study. Projects should reflect not only what you have done in response to class assignments, but what interests you about design."

**The portfolio should be as much an indication of what interests you, as it is a reflection of what you've done. If your concern relates to how design responds to audience differences for example, that concern should be evident in the work you show, regardless of the content of each piece in the portfolio.**
Meredith Davis, Head
Department of Graphic Design
North Carolina State University
Raleigh, NC

# Graphic Design
# Graduate Schools

California Institute of the Arts
2700 McBean Parkway
Valencia, CA 91355

Cranbrook Academy of Art
500 Lone Pine Road
Bloomfield Hills, MI 48013

Illinois Institute of Technology
Institute of Design
3360 South State Street
Chicago, IL 60616

North Carolina State University
School of Design
Raleigh, NC 27695-7701

Ohio State University
Department of Industrial Design
128 North Oval Mall
Columbus, OH 43210

Pratt Institute
School of Art and Design
200 Willoughby Avenue
Brooklyn, NY 11205

Rhode Island School of Design
2 College Street
Providence, RI 02903

Rochester Institute of Technology
College of Fine and Applied Arts
James Booth Building
Rochester, NY 14623-0887

Southeastern Massachusetts University
College of Visual and Performing Arts
North Dartmouth, MA 02747

University of Cincinnati
College of Design, Architecture, Planning
Cincinnati, OH 45221-0016

University of Illinois at Chicago
School of Art and Design
P.O. Box 4348
Chicago, IL 60680

University of Michigan
School of Art
2000 Bonisteel Blvd.
Ann Arbor, MI 48109

University of Texas
College of Fine Arts
Austin, TX 78712

University of Washington
School of Art
Seattle, WA 98195

Western Michigan University
College of Fine Arts
Kalamazoo, MI 49008

Virginia Commonwealth University
Communication Arts and Design
325 North Harrison Street
Richmond, VA 23284-2519

Yale University
School of Art
180 York Street
New Haven, CT 06520

Jan van Eyck Akademie
Academieplein 1
6211 KM Maastricht
The Netherlands

Kunstgewerbeschule Basel
Vogelsanstrasse 15
4000 Basel, Switzerland

Royal College of Art
Kensington Gore
London, S.W. 7, England

University of Alberta
Department of Art and Design
Edmonton T6G OX7 Canada

# Portfolio Renewal

The design portfolio should not be considered a static measure of your creativity at a single point in time. It is better viewed as an open ended system, changeable as your work evolves. If you are heavily involved in the interview process and a sample is attracting little attention or few positive comments, replace it with something more powerful. Act quickly even if it means late-night work. Strive to keep your creative portfolio current and ready to present on short notice.

As you gain design experience, plan to stockpile printed samples, tear sheets and transparencies from each project assigned. You will probably collect far more material than you will ultimately use to remodel your book. Yet if you neglect to gather samples very soon after printing or publication, the opportunity might be lost. Accumulate at least 10 printed samples of each relevant project. File them in or near your portfolio case for easy retrieval.

It is wise to keep organized files of trademarks, sketches, slides, comps and computer disks that reflect work process on interesting problems. Some wonderful creative solutions fail to reach printing or production yet might have portfolio potential. With your design development records at hand, raw ideas can be quickly converted to finished portfolio samples.

Designers typically progress through many distinct portfolios during a career. In addition to using your book for landing positions or projects, you will also find it useful to enter design competitions, conduct promotional activities and deliver professional presentations. Think of the creative portfolio as a reference bank on which you can draw to define your past, present and future.

**Think of the portfolio presentation as one of the most important design assignments you will have in school. The portfolio should be seen as an ongoing evolutionary process, in which you are regularly inserting new work and pulling out older, less effective examples.**
R. Roger Remington
Professor/Graphic Design
Rochester Institute
of Technology
Rochester, NY

**The field of Graphic Design is changing so quickly that the only constant in the field is change itself. Tools and skills that seem permanently valuable become meaningless overnight. Whatever you learn will become obsolete faster than you can discover what is making it obsolete. To remain competitive, you have to invest continually in skills and equipment. The price of the electronic devices needed just to stay in one place exceeds the earning capacity of the average designer. More work is done by fewer workers at lower wages, and the competition is fierce and getting fiercer. So, what's to do? Don't learn one thing and think that it's going to carry you. Learn how to learn, and take chances. If you're not afraid to fail, you have a higher likelihood of success. Don't be lukewarm. Don't give up too soon.**
David Lance Goines
Principal
Saint Hieronymus Press
Berkeley, CA

# Portfolio
# Checklist

**1** Does the portfolio show your best and most recent work?

**2** Is your craft impeccable and uncompromising?

**3** Does your book portray a unique design vision?

**4** Are your conceptual capabilities apparent?

**5** Have you included samples to show drawing competence?

**6** Do you show historical, experimental and technical typographic insight?

**7** Does the portfolio include evidence of your design process?

**8** Are your computer skills clearly demonstrated?

**9** Have you included evidence of prepress/production knowledge?

**10** Does your book integrate good writing with good design?

**11** Will your creative samples communicate as a system?

**12** Has your portfolio sequence been tested and refined?

**13** Can you target a variety of employers with your portfolio?

**14** Does your book show that you can begin work at a professional level?

**15** Does the portfolio predict that you will grow on the job?

# Portfolio Security

As you embark on your job search, consider the value and security of your portfolio. What is your finished book worth? The cost of a high quality case, mounting boards, transparencies, typesetting, camera work, color comprehensive materials, computer output, protective films and adhesives will range between $500 and $2500. A printed resume will add $200 or more. Not counting your many hours of labor, the finished portfolio becomes a very significant investment worth protecting.

Be sure to make at least two color slide versions of your portfolio. Photograph your work using a copystand. Frame each portfolio piece carefully with similar borders. Ektachrome film (E-6 processing) is appropriate. These color slide versions of your portfolio will prove handy for travel, provide back-up when your book is dropped off, and serve as insurance in case of disaster.

In addition to slide copies, it is wise to make a video record of your portfolio. For insurance purposes, the video should show the case closed, case open, identity tags or label and a quick view of your plates, resumes, sketchbooks, etc. Your goal here is to clearly document the dollar value of your book, not to assemble a creative video.

What can possibly happen to your portfolio? Theft, fire or shipping damage are most likely. Travel to an interview puts your book at risk . . . whenever it leaves your hands. Thefts are all too common in urban areas. When shipping your portfolio be sure to insure the full value of both case and contents. Loss of your portfolio will postpone your job search.

Insurance professionals recommend a telephone confirmation of specific policy coverage on your portfolio. Most renter and homeowner policies cover portfolio value in the same manner as luggage. Your portfolio is insured against theft providing the vehicle or room is secured with locked doors and windows and the case is reasonably concealed.

Clear identification both inside and on the exterior of the case will aid recovery. A locked case will help reinforce any claim. Evidence of "physical forced entry" confirmed in a police report will begin financial restitution. Automobile insurance with comprehensive coverage may also provide in-vehicle protection. Another alternative is to have a year-long portfolio "rider" attached to your existing policy.

It is prudent to keep good records of all portfolio and resume expenses. Insurance will reimburse only your physical loss of case and contents, but not the days or weeks spent to assemble your book. While a lost portfolio can deal a serious psychological setback to the young designer, proper insurance and back-up copies help soften the financial blow.

Having lost everything except a few samples in the Oakland firestorm of 1991, I recommend that you make a habit of routinely dropping samples of your work into a "quarterly envelope." Put a quarterly note in your datebook to remove all accumulated printed samples and slides to a location other than your office.

Leslie Becker
Associate Dean
School of Design
California College of
Arts and Crafts
San Francisco

# Portfolio Bibliography

Books, Boxes and Portfolios.
Franz Zeier.
New York:
Design Press.

Breaking into Advertising:
Making Your Portfolio Work for You.
Ken Musto.
New York:
Van Nostrand Reinhold.

Comping Techniques.
Suzanne West.
New York:
Watson-Guptill.

Graphic Design Career Guide.
James Craig.
New York:
Watson-Guptill.

How to Put Your Book Together
and Get a Job In Advertising.
Maxine Paetro.
New York:
Hawthorn Books.

How to Prepare Your Portfolio.
Ed Marquand.
New York:
Art Direction Books.

The Advertising Portfolio.
Ann Marie Barry.
Lincolnwood, IL:
NTC Publishing Group.

The Graphic Design Portfolio.
Paula Scher.
New York:
Watson-Guptill.

The Perfect Portfolio.
Henrietta Brackman.
New York:
Amphoto/Watson-Guptill.

The Ultimate Portfolio.
Martha Metzdorf.
Cincinnati:
North Light Books.

# Resume
# Bibliography

Designing Creative Resumes.
Gregg Berryman.
Menlo Park, CA:
Crisp Publications.

Beyond the Resume.
Herman Holz.
New York:
McGraw-Hill.

How to Write Better Resumes.
Adele Lewis.
New York:
Barrons.

Resume Writing.
Burdette Bostwick.
New York:
John Wiley & Sons.

Resumes for Advertising Careers.
Editors of VGM Career Horizons.
Lincolnwood, IL:
NTC Publishing Group.

Resumes for Hard Times.
Bob Weinstein.
New York:
Simon and Schuster.

The Perfect Resume.
Tom Jackson.
Garden City, NY:
Anchor Press/Doubleday.

# Self-Marketing Bibliography

Becoming a Designer.
Mark Isaacson.
Arcata, CA:
Impact Studio.

Careers by Design.
Roz Goldfarb.
New York:
Allworth Press.

Creative Self-Promotion
on a Limited Budget.
Sally Prince Davis.
Cincinnati:
North Light Books.

Design Career.
S. Heller/L. Talarico.
New York:
Van Nostrand Reinhold.

Dress for Success.
John T. Molloy.
New York:
Warner Books, Inc.

Getting Hired.
Edward Rogers.
Englewood Cliffs, NJ:
Prentice-Hall Inc.

Promo Series.
Rose DeNeve.
Cincinnati:
North Light Books.

Self Promotion Annuals.
How Magazine.
Cincinnati:
North Light Books.

The Art and Business
of Creative Self-Promotion.
J. Herring/M. Fulton.
New York:
Watson-Guptill.

The School of Visual
Arts Guide to Careers.
Dee Ito
New York:
Visual Arts Press.

# Portfolio Sources

Brewer-Cantelmo
116 East 27th Street
New York, NY 10016

Century Archival Products
2419 East Franklin Street
Richmond, VA 23223

Charrette
31 Olympia Avenue
Woburn, MA 01888

Custom Case Company
1049 Wall Street
Los Angeles, CA 90015

H. G. Daniels Co.
2543 West Sixth Street
Los Angeles, CA 90057

Faber Castell
551 Springplace Road
Lewisburg, TN 37091

Flax Art & Design
1699 Market Street
San Francisco, CA 94120

A. I. Friedman
25 West 45th Street
New York, NY 10036

Joshua Meier Corp.
7401 West Side Avenue
North Bergen, NJ 07047

Susan Noell, Casemaker
5333 Nakoma
Dallas, TX 75209

Summit Travelware
11278 Goss Street
Sun Valley, CA 91352

University Arts
267 Hamilton Avenue
Palo Alto, CA 94301

*Archival materials*
Light Impressions
P.O. Box 940
Rochester, NY 14603

*Colorprints from slides*
The Slideprinter
P.O. Box 9506
Denver, CO 80209

*Electronic PortfolioMaker*®
CRIT
P.O. Box 18808
Baltimore, MD 21206

*Specialty papers*
Paper Direct
205 Chubb Avenue
Lyndhurst, NJ 07071

*Exotic papers, boards*
Vicki Schober Company
2363 North Mayfair Road
Milwaukee, WI 53226

*Plastic sheets*
TAP Plastics
4538 Auburn Blvd.
Sacramento, CA 95841

*Portfolio laminator*
Azevedo's Laminating Inc.
165 Commerce Circle
Sacramento, CA 95815

*Slide storage products*
Reliance Plastics
217 Brook Avenue
Passaic, NJ 07055

*Slide storage products*
20th Century Plastics
3628 Crenshaw Blvd.
Los Angeles, CA 90016

*Specialty papers*
Paper Access
23 West 18th Street
New York, NY 10011

# Placement
# Agencies

Edwards & Shepard Agency
1170 Broadway
New York, NY 10001

Jerry Fields Associates
353 Lexington Avenue
New York, NY 10016

Roz Goldfarb Associates
10 E 22nd Street
New York, NY 10010

Janou Pakter Inc.
91 Fifth Avenue
New York, NY 10003

Cheryl Roshak & Co.
141 Fifth Avenue
New York, NY 10010

RitaSue Siegel Associates
18 East 48th Street
New York, NY 10017

Stone & Co.
Forbes Business Center
222 Forbes Road
Braintree, MA 02184

T-Square etc.
1990 South Bundy Drive
Los Angeles, CA 90025

American Center for Design
233 East Ontario Street
Chicago, IL 60611

American Institute of Graphic Arts
1059 Third Avenue
New York, NY 10021

Graphic Artists Guild
11 West 20th Street
New York, NY 10011

International Design by
Electronics Association
2200 Wilson Blvd.
Arlington, VA 22201

Magazine Industry Market Place
R. R. Bowker Company
245 West 17th Street
New York, NY 10011

Places Rated Almanac.
R. Boyer & D. Savageau.
New York:
Prentice Hall

Society of Environmental
Graphic Designers
47 Third Street
Cambridge, MA 02141

Society of Publication Designers
60 East 42nd Street
New York, NY 10165

Standard Directory of
Advertising Agencies
866 Third Avenue
New York, NY 10022

The Creative Blackbook
115 Fifth Avenue
New York, NY 10003

The Livable Cities Almanac.
John Tepper Marlin.
New York:
Harper Perennial.

The Workbook
940 North Highland Avenue
Los Angeles, CA 90038